Learn to Dance

Learn to Dance

A Step-by-Step Guide to Ballroom and Latin Dances

COLETTE REDGRAVE

First published by Parragon in 2008

Parragon
Queen Street House
4 Queen Street
Bath BA1 1HE, UK

Designed, produced, and packaged by
Stonecastle Graphics Limited

Text by Colette Redgrave
Designed by Paul Turner and Sue Pressley
Editorial consultant: Nick Freeth
Edited by Philip de Ste. Croix
Ballroom dancers: Bella Verrechia and Tom Verrechia
Latin dancers: Robert John Coombs and Jodie Tolhurst
Dance consultant: Mark Shutlar

ISBN 978-1-4075-3904-1

Printed in China

Picture credits:
All photography by Roddy Paine with the exception of the following:
© Corbis: 46 (left); Barney Burstein © Burstein Collection/Corbis 6 (above); © Christie's Images/ Corbis 6 (below), 22 (left); © Sunset Boulevard/ Corbis 22 (right).
© Shutterstock.com: Tina Gill 54 (left).

Contents

Introduction 6

Getting Started 8

What to Wear 10

Music and Etiquette 12

Warming Up and Posture 14

Footwork 16

Dance Holds 18

Ballroom Dances 20

Ballroom: an Overview 22

The Waltz 24

Conventional Waltz Steps – 1 26

Conventional Waltz Steps – 2 28

Viennese Waltz Steps – 1 30

Viennese Waltz Steps – 2 32

The Foxtrot 34

Social or Rhythm Foxtrot Steps – 1 36

Social or Rhythm Foxtrot Steps – 2 38

The Tango 40

Tango Steps – 1 42

Tango Steps – 2 44

The Quickstep 46

Quickstep Steps – 1 48

Quickstep Steps – 2 50

Latin American Dances 52

Latin American Overview 54

The Rumba 56

Rumba Steps – 1 58

Rumba Steps – 2 60

Rumba Steps – 3 62

The Cha Cha 64

Cha Cha Steps – 1 66

Cha Cha Steps – 2 68

Cha Cha Steps – 3 71

Cha Cha Steps – 4 73

The Samba 74

Samba Steps – 1 76

Samba Steps – 2 77

The Salsa 80

Salsa Steps – 1 82

Salsa Steps – 2 84

Salsa Steps – 3 86

The Paso Doble 88

Paso Doble Steps – 1 90

Paso Doble Steps – 2 92

Index 96

Introduction

It is safe to say that more people enjoy dance today than ever before. Thanks to a fitness boom, and the endorsement of stars appearing on TV dance competition programs, dance exercise is currently one of the most phenomenal growth areas of 21st-century sport and social culture.

Dance is both a convenient and enjoyable form of physical activity, and a mental workout, engaging mind and body in harmony. It has also stood the test of time, and remains central to almost every national culture. We have all danced, or will dance, at some stage in our lives, be it during our childhood, teens or adulthood; we will dance at weddings and birthdays, and to mark success and achievement.

Historically, the act of dancing has also stirred up controversy and even outrage, with the close hold of the waltz (declared 'immoral and vulgar' in the 18th century) and the supposed 'obscenities' of the tango in the early 1900s challenging the conventions of acceptable public behavior in their respective eras. Today, disco and club culture may rival the more traditional pleasures of the ballroom; but while 'street style' hip-hop and Latin crazes continue to grow in popularity, increasing numbers of couples are looking to the dance floor for opportunities to be sexy, intimate, and flirtatious away from the bedroom in salsa bars and dance halls!

Above and above right: For centuries, the dance floor has blended formality with the more intimate thrill of close personal contact.

Although the professionals make it look incredibly easy, if you have witnessed the trials and tribulations of the celebrity participants in shows such as *Dancing With the Stars* then you may already have some appreciation of the hard work that dance involves.

This book aims to help you master its fundamentals: it introduces a selection of social ballroom dances and Latin styles, covers the warm-up exercises essential to dance practice and the basic hold positions for partnered dances, and offers advice on how to develop your skills. Step-by-step photographs and diagrams will give you the confidence and technical know-how to enjoy participating in classes or social dances, enabling you to 'let go' and enjoy the moment!

Getting Started

Think Ballroom, and you most probably think glamorous dresses, high heels, smart tuxedos, and possibly fake tans! In recent years, however, there have been huge advances in the design of dancers' outfits: their clothes are now fashionable in appearance, yet lightweight and washable, while their shoes are more comfortable and flexible than ever before. Thanks to the variety of the styles on offer, you can add your own identity to your dancing through what you wear.

This chapter looks at the correct clothing and footwear for Ballroom and Latin dancing, and gives you advice on choosing your first pair of ballroom shoes. It also tells you what you need to know about music and rhythm, and the principles of ballroom etiquette and safety – information which, when you've absorbed it, will allow you to attack your dance steps with assurance and enjoyment.

What to Wear

Clothing for dancing depends entirely on the venue or function you are attending. Comfort, however, should always prevail. For dance classes, you require clothes that allow you to move freely from the hips and do not hinder movement around the legs. Ladies will often choose to wear skirts that are appropriate to the style of dance, and men pants that are not restrictive. Feeling at ease is of the utmost importance, especially whilst learning.

Footwear

When starting out you may feel happy simply wearing a pair of your own shoes. However, trainers are not ideal for Ballroom or Latin except when dancing Swing or Jive styles, and sling-backs for ladies should be avoided. Ballroom shoes are specifically designed to make it easy to get around a dance floor. They are lightweight and comfortable, and will have a non-slip suede sole. Suede is malleable, and allows you to maintain some connection with the floor. As a beginner you are unlikely to require more than a single pair of shoes, but it is advisable to invest in well-made ones that provide good support.

Ladies

When choosing your first pair of shoes, consider a smaller heel to assist with balance and maintain confidence. A 2 or 2½ inch (5 or 6cm) heel height is advisable. Beginner ladies would do well to choose open-toed shoes that suit both Ballroom and Latin styles. A T-bar may help give more support.

Men's Ballroom shoes with 1 inch (2.5cm) heels.

Men's Latin Cuban heel shoes.

Men

Traditionally, men's shoes are almost always black. As with ladies' shoes, heel heights vary from 1 to 2 inches (2.5 to 5cm). Latin shoes that have a 'Cuban heel' can be uncomfortable and difficult to lead in when first learning steps. Patent shoes look sharp and smart for Ballroom, but may squeak or stick as they pass each other, and can crack with age. A suede, nubuck, or leather upper would be more practical for a beginner.

Ladies' Latin sandals with open toes.

Ladies' Latin sandals with open toes.

Ladies' Latin sandals with closed toes.

Ladies' Ballroom court shoes with straps.

Useful tip

Shoes often stretch over time. They also stretch more whilst dancing and shrink again when they cool!

Fit

Ballroom shoes should feel tighter than a 'normal' shoe. This is because they are made from very soft materials and will stretch and mold to your feet over time. When trying them on, they should be snug and supportive around your foot and should not slip at the back, or have space at the front of the toes as is usual with everyday shoes.

Reflections on dance

'Dancing is the loftiest, the most moving, the most beautiful of the arts, because it is not mere translation or abstraction from life; it is life itself.'

Henry Havelock Ellis (1859-1939)

Left and below: Wear clothes that feel comfortable and that you are free to dance in. Ladies may wear pants that allow easy movement.

Reflections on dance

'I did everything Fred (Astaire) did – in high heels and backward.'

Ginger Rogers (1911-1995)

Music and Etiquette

As a dancer you must be able to hear the rhythm that underlies any melody in order to identify the style of dance suited to an item of music. With practice and experience you will recognize the difference between the various dance rhythms, and be able to take to the floor with confidence.

Typically the **beat** of a musical piece is the 'drum beat' played by the percussion section. A group of these beats is identified as a 'bar' and a group of 'bars' is a 'phrase.' You will need to know how many beats per bar are used in typical Ballroom and Latin dances in order to identify them.

For example, you will probably instantly recognize 3/4 time (which has three beats per bar) as being a waltz, whose heavy first beat is followed by two lighter beats (*1* 2 3, *1* 2 3 etc.). Other dances are associated with 2/4 and 4/4 time:

Tango: 2 beats per bar (2/4)
Quickstep: 4 beats per bar (4/4)
Foxtrot: 4 beats per bar (4/4)
Samba: 2 beats per bar (2/4)
Rumba: 4 beats per bar (4/4)
Cha Cha: 4 beats per bar (4/4)
Salsa: 4 beats per bar (4/4)
Paso Doble: 2 beats per bar (2/4)

Tempo is simply the speed at which the music is played. In social dancing, most dances that are either in 4/4 or 2/4 are flexible and can be adapted to almost any tempo, but certain steps are restricted by the speed at which they can be performed.

We count each dance in a series of **Slows** and **Quicks**. The Slow is worth 2 beats in a bar of 4 beats and the Quick is worth just 1 beat in a bar of 4 beats.

 Throughout the book you will see this symbol suggesting songs/tracks suitable for the dance style it accompanies.

The following symbols have been used throughout the step-by-step instructions to denote:

 Man  Lady

Above: Music provides the inspiration and impetus for all your movements on the dance floor.

Etiquette

As a dancer it is important to know the direction in which you should travel around a dance floor and how to negotiate corners and other dancers. Many social dances are now performed in a variety of venues, such as restaurants, clubs, or hotels, but, as at competition level, avoiding other couples and obstacles is still very much a challenge.

If you are passing another couple, then it is your responsibility to avoid contact with them. Quite often it will be the more experienced dancers that are able to get past effortlessly, given the wider variety of steps available to them; however, no matter how confident or expert you are, squeezing past when there just isn't enough room is frowned upon.

The diagram below illustrates the direction in which you should move around the dance floor.

Wall
Facing wall
Against line of dance
Line of dance
Wall
Facing center
Against line of dance
Line of dance
Line of dance
Center of the room
Diagonal to center
Diagonal to wall
Facing center
Facing wall
Against line of dance

Above: Knowing your position and direction on the dance floor gives you the assurance you need to dance with confidence.

Left: This diagram indicates the correct direction in which dancers should move around the room.

Reflections on dance

'And those who were seen dancing were thought to be insane by those who could not hear the music.'

Friedrich Wilhelm Nietzsche (1844-1900)

Useful tip

If you collide with another couple, simply apologize and move on. Temperamental outbursts on the dance floor should be avoided, and handling the situation with courtesy is the professional approach!

Beginners will generally move more slowly round the floor – this is to be expected. Do not be afraid to move slightly closer to the center of the room in order to allow plenty of space for more competent dancers to pass you. This way you will avoid collisions.

Warming Up and Posture

As with all physical exercise, it is best to do some basic warm-ups before launching yourself into the dances themselves. Of course, your social setting might determine whether or not you are able to do this, but whilst practicing, try to become accustomed to gently loosening and stretching the major muscles in preparation for your dancing, using the exercises shown here.

Neck and shoulders

Gently rotate the shoulders forward and backward, loosening the neck muscles. Shrug them up and down, really releasing and letting go on the downward movement. Repeat 5 to 10 times in each direction.

Tip your head over toward the left shoulder and hold for 10 seconds. Repeat on the right.

Hips

Rotate the hips in a clockwise and counterclockwise movement. In order to do this freely, stand with your legs just wider than hip width apart and bend the knees slightly. Keep the knees loose, and rotate the hips as if swinging a hula hoop around your waist. Repeat 5 to 10 times in both directions.

Knees

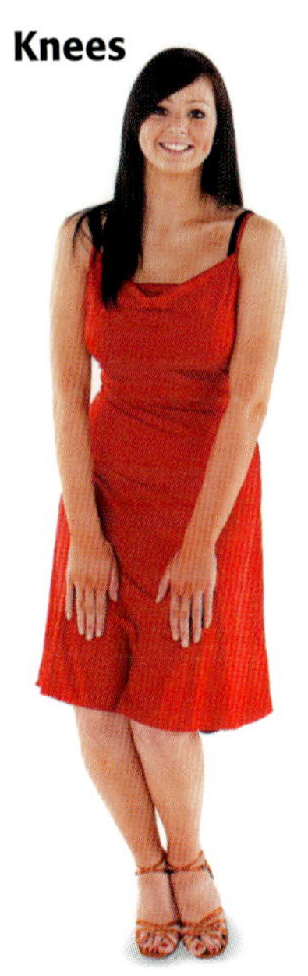

With your feet slightly apart, place your hands on your thighs. Gently bend your knees and then move them in a circular motion clockwise and counterclockwise. Repeat this exercise 5 to 10 times in each direction.

When attempting the next two exercises, you may wish to hold onto the back of a chair to maintain your balance at first.

Ankles

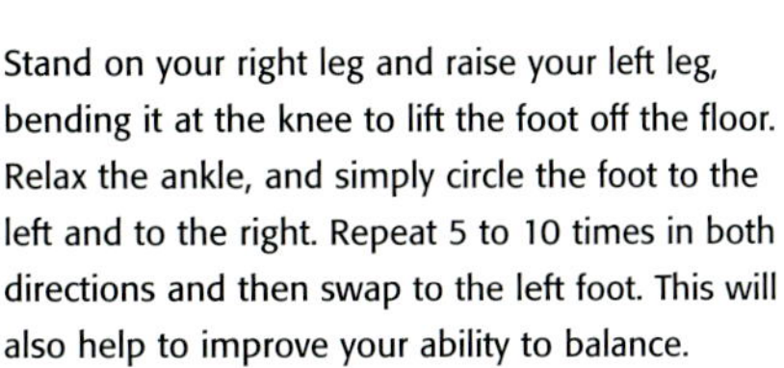

Stand on your right leg and raise your left leg, bending it at the knee to lift the foot off the floor. Relax the ankle, and simply circle the foot to the left and to the right. Repeat 5 to 10 times in both directions and then swap to the left foot. This will also help to improve your ability to balance.

Rising onto the balls of the feet

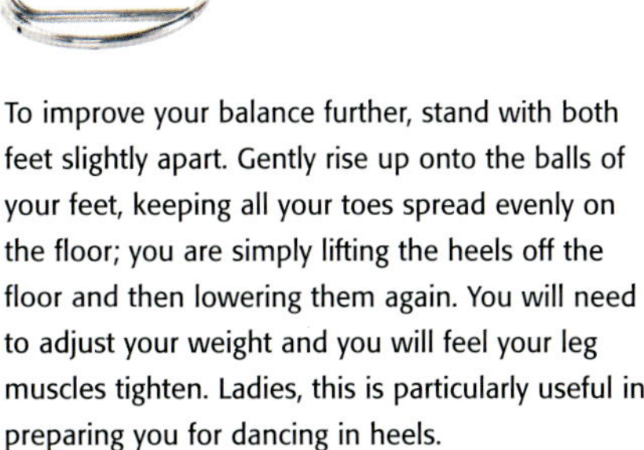

To improve your balance further, stand with both feet slightly apart. Gently rise up onto the balls of your feet, keeping all your toes spread evenly on the floor; you are simply lifting the heels off the floor and then lowering them again. You will need to adjust your weight and you will feel your leg muscles tighten. Ladies, this is particularly useful in preparing you for dancing in heels.

Posture

One of the defining features of a professional ballroom dancer is his or her posture. Good posture and stance distinguishes the experienced participant from the beginner. You will feel more confident and in control of a dance by working on your posture and strength; the gentleman especially must provide a strong framework onto which the lady can take hold. Posture will improve both the look and feel of your dancing.

Good posture

Stand with your back to a flat area of wall. Pull in your stomach muscles tightly, and lift your shoulders up and back to make contact with the wall. Now stand away from the wall maintaining this position. Relax, but keep your stomach held in and shoulders back.

Bad posture

Whilst dancing, you will inevitably move more freely, but as you improve, you will find that the more you maintain your posture, the stronger and more grounded you will become. This in turn will help your balance and sense of connection with both your partner and the floor.

Footwork

Footwork is used to describe the part of the foot in contact with the floor at any one time. Throughout this book, we will refer to the following footwork positions. Look back to these photographs if you're in any doubt of where your feet should be.

Firstly, you must be able to identify the different parts of the foot:

Ball is used to describe the pad underneath the foot on which we spread our weight evenly.

Flat is used to describe the foot when standing naturally, with both the ball and heel making contact with the floor.

Heel refers to the heel of the foot.

Toe refers to the toes.

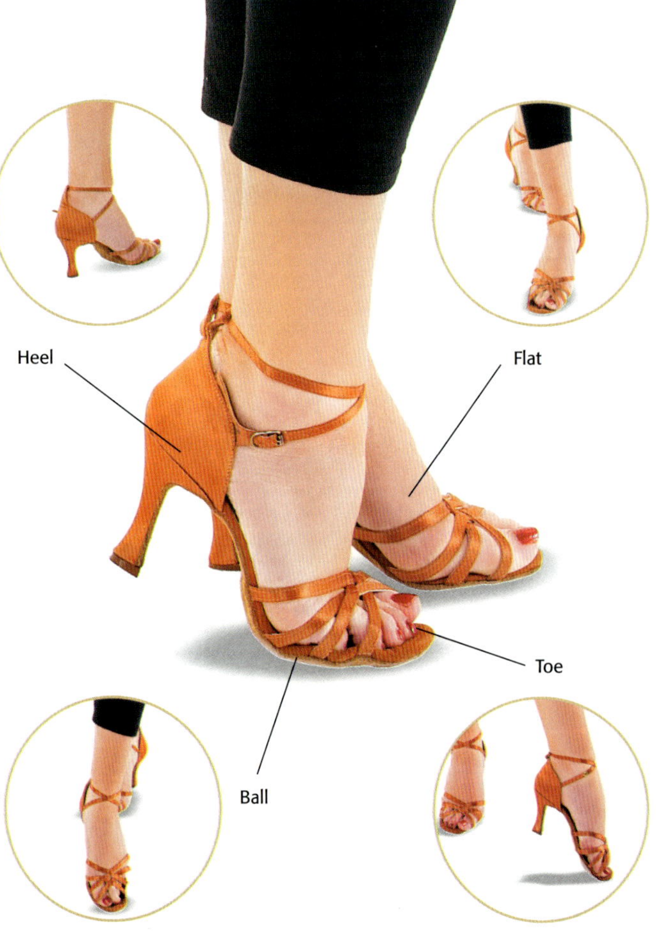

Steps

A step is simply a natural step! Most ballroom steps, however, are **heel lead** or **toe lead**.

Traveling forward, the heel will make contact with the floor first. This is a **heel lead**.

When traveling backward, the toe will make contact with the floor first. This is a **toe lead**.

The toe lead is slightly harder than the heel lead as it is not as natural. Extend the toes from the ankle as you step backward, as if feeling for the floor with your toes before the rest of the foot lands.

Ball-flats: In the Latin dances the majority of the steps will be 'ball-flat' movements. This is when the ball makes contact with the floor first, followed by the rest of the foot in a continuous movement.

Ball-taps: A 'ball-tap' is usually preceded by a step. As the name suggests, the ball of one foot taps the floor adjacent to the opposite foot.

Hips

The hips are only used in the Latin dance section. They accompany the 'ball-flat' movement giving the Latin dances their characteristic sexy motion.

The correct hip action in Latin is achieved by allowing the weight to settle into the standing leg onto which you've just stepped.

Dance Holds

Nearly all Ballroom dances are performed in a standard ballroom hold (with the exception of the Tango), whereas the Latin dances are performed in a more relaxed ballroom hold. They also incorporate the open face position (see page 19). The following photographs demonstrate how these positions should be taken up; refer back to them when commencing each dance.

Standard ballroom hold

1 The man holds his left hand at eye level.

2 The lady hooks her right hand lightly over the man's, and clasps lightly together – a feeling like that of a light, but firm, handshake.

3 The man places his right hand on the lady's shoulder blade. This right arm provides the supportive framework in which the lady will dance.

4 The lady places her left hand on the man's right arm, just below the shoulder in the groove of the arm muscle.

5 The lady stands slightly offset from the man's center: i.e. the center of his body.

Tango hold

1

The man's right hand is placed slightly lower and farther round the lady's back to enable the lady to place her left hand with its palm facing down underneath the man's right arm.

2

3

This in turn brings the man's right side closer to the lady's right.

Open face position

The man offers his left hand to the lady, while keeping his elbow close to the side of his body.

The lady places her right hand on top of the man's left, also keeping her elbow close to her right side, and clasping his hand. Keep this position relaxed.

Latin hold

1

Closed hold

Assume the ballroom hold position and simply relax it. Step a little away from each other and relax at the elbows.

2

Side by side

As used in the 'New Yorks' (see page 60) and also known as the 'open promenade' position.

Ballroom Dances

Ballroom dancing is an extraordinarily enduring social pastime. Its origins lie in the palaces of Renaissance Europe, and it owes its longevity to the timeless grace, splendor, and refinement it epitomizes – and to its ability to absorb later innovations by performers on both sides of the Atlantic, including those of 20th-century greats like Fred Astaire and Ginger Rogers.

More recently, movies such as Dirty Dancing *and* Strictly Ballroom*, as well as numerous elaborately choreographed stage shows, have inspired and enthralled a new generation of dancers. However, the principal driving force behind the contemporary ballroom dancing scene is probably television. In 2003, UK broadcaster BBC responded to a wave of demand for celebrity-based entertainment by re-inventing its venerable ballroom TV show* Come Dancing *(first seen back in 1949, but dropped in 1995) as* Strictly Come Dancing. *Featuring a competing cast of famous names, it generated huge viewing figures, and its format has since enjoyed massive success in the USA and throughout the world under the title of* Dancing With the Stars. *The program's popularity has played a key role in raising public awareness of the beauty, elegance, and sheer entertainment that ballroom dancing can provide.*

Ballroom: an Overview

Ballroom dancing competitions have been held since 1909, when a Frenchman, Camille de Rhynal, established an annual 'World Championship' in Paris. The 'Ballroom' category includes the Waltz in both its slow (Conventional) and faster (Viennese) forms, the Slow Foxtrot, the Quickstep, and the Tango. Latin styles such as the Rumba and the Jive, as well as Old Time and sequence dancing, were originally classed as 'Ballroom' too – but were excluded from the 'Modern Ballroom' genre that emerged later. 'Modern Ballroom' was eventually renamed 'Standard Ballroom' by Europeans to avoid confusion with the 'jazz' style of dancing that developed in the 1920s.

In the USA, the term 'International Standard' was used for what was known elsewhere as 'Standard Ballroom.' Alongside it, an 'American Smooth' dance technique evolved in the Land of the Free. 'American Smooth' style applies to the Waltz, Viennese Waltz, Tango, and Foxtrot, and allows for more freedom of expression than its European counterpart, with open holds, 'apart' positions and even lifts. It was epitomized by the classic routines of Fred Astaire and Ginger Rogers, choreographed by Astaire himself or Hermes Pan.

The roots of Ballroom lie in the formal dances that were once the exclusive province of a wealthy and powerful elite: the Volta, a dance involving high jumps and turns, which appeared in the 16th century, and (later) the Waltz were all the rage in the Royal Courts of Europe, and went on to spread throughout high society. Today, though, the experience of dancing to music is open to everyone, and this chapter will unlock its delights as it explains the basic steps required to perform the Waltz, Foxtrot, Tango, and Quickstep.

Above: Fred Astaire and Ginger Rogers, Hollywood's most celebrated dancing couple. Left: An elegant European 'salon de danse.' *Opposite: The Waltz is an all-time favorite among dancers of any age.*

The Waltz

Surprisingly, considering their rather risqué backgrounds and controversial beginnings, the Waltz and the Tango are the only Ballroom dances that have retained the original steps that they featured in the days of the first Paris championships. Even that other 'hardy perennial,' the Slow Foxtrot, has changed markedly in execution since the early 1900s.

With its origins in peasant dances, the Waltz first found popularity in areas of southern Germany and Austria – and especially in Vienna – during the 17th and 18th century. Later, its fame spread to Britain, where its 'close hold' performing position and the rapid turning it demanded were a source of outrage and fierce criticism in some quarters. A ball in London in 1816, hosted by the Prince Regent, at which a number of aristocrats danced the Waltz provoked the following stern outburst in *The Times* newspaper: 'So long as this obscene display was confined to prostitutes and adulteresses, we did not think it deserving of notice; but now that it is attempted to be forced on the respectable classes of society by the civil examples of their superiors, we feel it a duty to warn every parent against exposing his daughter to so fatal a contagion.'

The Waltz's American debut in 1834 – as part of a display given in Boston, Massachusetts by one of the city's leading dance teachers, Lorenzo Papanti – drew similar condemnation. However, within a few decades, the US public, like dance lovers in Europe before them, had been won over by the dance, and it has remained a firm favorite ever since.

Opposite: This couple execute their Waltz steps with vigor and passion.

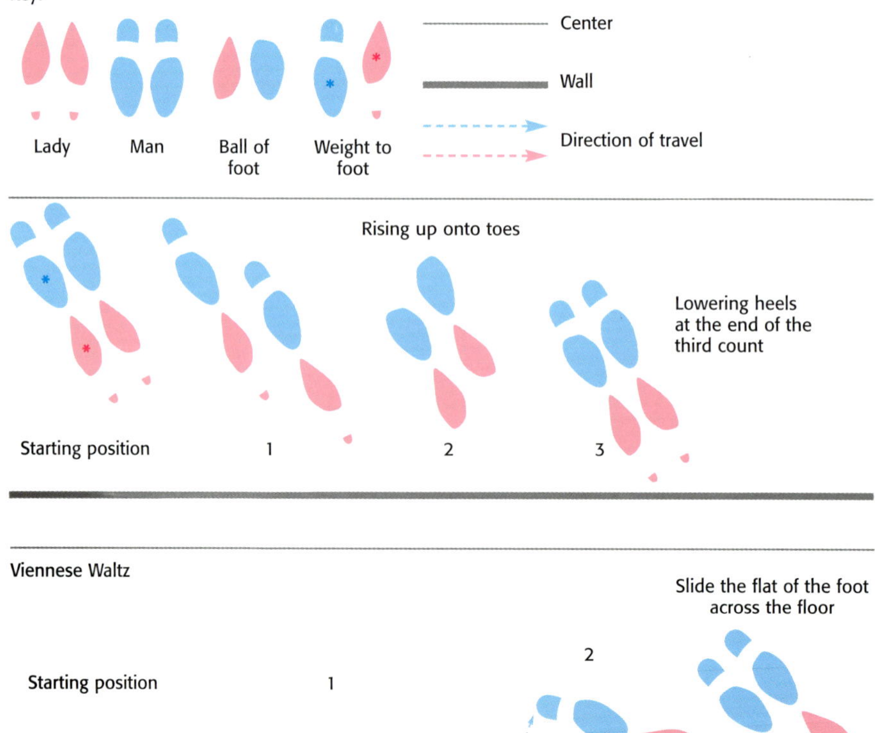

Waltz Facts

- **noun** a dance in triple time (i.e. with three beats to the bar) performed by a couple, who turn rhythmically round and round as they progress around the dance floor.
- **verb 1** dance a Waltz. **2** move or act lightly, casually, or inconsiderately.

Origin of name: German *Walzer*, from *walzen*: 'revolve'

Mood: elegant, classy, nostalgic, English, romantic, weddings

Time: 3/4

Basic count: 1, 2, 3

Beats per bar: 3

Tempo: 28–30 bars per minute

Hold position: standard ballroom hold

Suggested track: *Moon River* by Andy Williams

Conventional Waltz Steps – 1

Left foot closed change or reverse to natural

Man begins facing diagonal to the outside wall. Weight should be in the right foot, ready to move off with the left.

Lady begins with her back diagonal to the outside wall. Weight should be in the left foot, ready to move off with the right.

The Waltz has a distinct sense of rise and fall in it. Imagine you are following the curve shown below: your 'peak and trough' is made by the rise and fall from the toes to the flat of the foot, assisted by the knees. At the end of each bar (of 1, 2, 3), soften your knees and lower the heels. The first beat of the bar is the heaviest step, and is emphasized by bending the knees as you launch yourself up into the step onto the toes. You should always be rising on counts 2 and 3, and starting to fall again at the end of the count of 3 leading into the 1. Keep this motion fluid at all times.

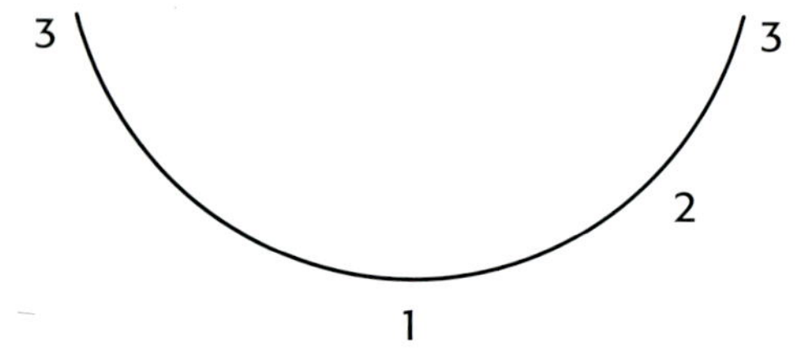

1

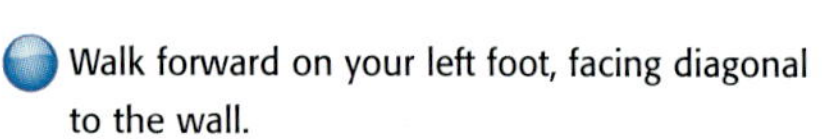

Walk forward on your left foot, facing diagonal to the wall.

Walk backward on your right foot, backing diagonal to the wall.

2

Step forward on the right foot onto your toes – as your right foot passes your left, the heel naturally releases, so that you rise up onto your toes on both feet.

Walk backward on your left foot, leading with the toe, backing diagonal to the wall, and rising onto your toes at the same time as the man.

3

Close your left foot to your right, on your toes, facing diagonal to the wall. Lower at the end of the third count, dropping your heels and relaxing the knees slightly.

Close your right foot to your left, on your toes, facing diagonal to the center. Lower at the end of the third count, dropping your heels and relaxing the knees slightly.

Natural turn – six steps are used to complete the turn: 1, 2, 3, 1, 2, 3

1

Step forward on the right foot – introducing a rotation in the upper body, felt through the shoulders as if you were pushing forward with the left hand.

Left foot steps backward, backing diagonally to the wall.

2

At this point the man is backing diagonal to the center.

The left foot then moves forward and slightly to the side. Just as the feet pass, allow the body to continue turning, placing the left foot to the side of the right.

Place the right foot to the right side, and swing it open, pointing down the line of dance.

3

Lower at the end of the third count, lowering your heels and relaxing the knees slightly.

Close the right foot to left whilst up on your toes, completing the turn by ending up with your back facing down the line of dance. Lower at the end of the third count, lowering your heels, and relaxing the knees slightly.

Close your left foot to right whilst up on your toes, completing the turn by ending up facing down the line of dance.

1

Left foot now steps backward, toe leading, down the line of dance.

Right foot steps forward down the line of dance, heel leading, allowing the left side of the body to move forward.

2

Step your right foot to your right side, pointing your toes diagonal to center. Body turns less to face center.

Place the left foot to the left side, with your body backing center.

3

Lower at the end of the third count, lowering your heels and relaxing the knees slightly.

Close your left foot to your right facing diagonal to center, with the same feeling of rise and fall. Lower at the end of the third count, lowering your heels and relaxing the knees slightly.

Close your right foot to your left, backing diagonal center, allowing a little extra turn so that you end up with your back facing diagonal center. Same feeling of rise and fall as before.

Conventional Waltz Steps – 2

Right foot closed change or natural to reverse

1

- Walk forward on your right foot, facing diagonal to the center.
- Walk backward on your left foot, backing diagonal to the center.

2

It is often taught that this step should be taken to the side. However, due to the forward traveling motion of the waltz, you will probably step forward and slightly to the side as described below, dependent on your ability to move in relation to the couples around you.

- Step forward and slightly to the side on the left foot onto your toes. As your left foot passes your right, the heel naturally releases so that you rise up onto your toes on both feet.
- Walk backward and slightly to the side on your right foot, leading with the toe, backing diagonal to the wall, and rising at the same time as the man onto your toes.

3

- Close your right foot to your left, on your toes, facing diagonal to the center.
  Lower at the end of the third count, lowering your heels and relaxing the knees slightly.
- Close your left foot to your right, on your toes, backing diagonal to the center.
  Lower at the end of the third count, lowering your heels and relaxing the knees slightly.

Suggested choreography: one left foot closed change, one natural turn, one right foot closed change, and one reverse turn – repeated as many times as required!

Reverse turn

1

- Step your left foot forward, facing diagonal center, preparing to turn left.
- Step your right foot back, diagonal to center, preparing to turn left.

2

- Step your right foot to your right side, backing diagonal to the wall.
- Step your left foot to your left side, facing diagonal to the wall.

3

- Close your left foot to your right, backing the line of dance (LOD).
- Close your right foot to your left, facing down the line of dance (LOD).

4

- Step your right foot back along the LOD, preparing to turn left.
- Step your left foot forward along LOD, preparing to turn left.

5

- Step your left foot to your left side, keeping your body facing toward the wall.
- Step your right foot to your right side, backing the wall.

6

- Close your right foot to your left, on your toes, facing diagonal to the wall. Lower at the end of the third count, lowering your heels and relaxing your knees slightly.
- Close your left foot to your right, on your toes, facing diagonal to the wall. Lower at the end of the third count, lowering your heels and relaxing your knees slightly.

Viennese Waltz Steps – 1

The main difference between the Viennese Waltz and the Conventional Waltz is that the former is danced at nearly double the speed of the latter. The other dissimilarity is that there is no rise and fall in the Viennese, whose dancers appear almost to glide across the floor. When closing the feet, try to avoid rising onto the toes; instead, close the foot, moving onto the flat.

A further interesting feature of the Viennese is that the lady always performs exactly the same steps as the man, but at different times. As the man performs steps 1, 2, and 3, the lady performs the steps that he would execute on counts 4, 5, and 6 – and vice versa.

The feet remain flat on the floor throughout the Viennese Waltz, closing together without lifting the heels off the floor.

Natural turn

Reflections on dance

'There are short-cuts to happiness, and dancing is one of them.'

Vicki Baum (1888-1960)

- Man begins down the line of dance with his weight in his left foot, ready to move off with the right.
- Lady begins by backing the line of dance with her weight in her right foot, ready to move off with her left.

Special tip: You should maintain an awareness of your body in relation to the wall, and center of the dance floor, each time you step to the side.

1

- Right foot steps forward with a heel lead, allowing the upper body to turn to the right – it should do this naturally.
- Left foot steps backward down the LOD with a toe lead.

2

- (Man) Step to the side with your left foot – toe lead.
- (Lady) Step your right foot to your right side, pointing your toes diagonal to center. Body turns less to face center.

3

- (Man) Close your right foot to your left – sliding the flat of the foot across the floor. Man ends up backing diagonal center.
- (Lady) Close your left foot to your right – sliding the flat of the foot across the floor. Lady ends up facing diagonal center.

4

- (Man) Left foot steps backward down the LOD with a toe lead.
- (Lady) Right foot steps forward with a heel lead, allowing the upper body to turn naturally to the right.

5

- (Man) Step your right foot to your right side, pointing your toes diagonal to center. Body turns less to face center.
- (Lady) Step to side with your left foot – toe lead.

6

Viennese Waltz Facts

Mood: elegant, flowing, spinning, fast, think Austria

Time: 3/4

Basic count: 1, 2, 3

Beats per bar: 3

Tempo: 58-60 bars per minute

Hold position: close hold

Suggested track: *The Blue Danube* by Johann Strauss II

- (Man) Close your left foot to your right – sliding the flat of the foot across the floor. Man ends up facing diagonal center.
- (Lady) Close your right foot to your left – sliding the flat of the foot across the floor.

(Man and Lady) As man and lady close, they should prepare to take the first step again down the LOD.

Viennese Waltz Steps – 2

Reverse turn

Turning tip: Change steps are not advisable on corners, as they can be confusing. Add an extra natural or reverse turn in order to negotiate the corner. Ladies should take this from the man's lead – it's up to you, guys!

Suggested choreography: Try four of the natural turns followed by a forward change step, and then four reverse turns and a change step to commence the natural turns again.

1
- Left foot steps down the line of dance – the heel leads, allowing the upper body to turn slightly to the left.
- Right foot steps backward down the LOD.

2
- Step your right foot to your right side – toe leads back to the wall.
- Step your left foot to your left side, body facing the wall – toes pointing diagonal to the wall.

3
- Cross your left foot in front of your right standing on the toes with your back diagonal to the wall – slide your toes across the floor.
- Close your right foot to your left by sliding your right foot on the flat into your left.

4
- Right foot steps backward down the LOD.
- Left foot steps forward down the LOD – heel lead, allowing the upper body to turn slightly to the left.

5

- Step your left foot to your left side, with your body facing the wall – while your toes are pointing diagonal to the wall.
- Step your right foot to your right side – toe lead, backing the wall.

6

- Close your right foot to your left by sliding your right foot on the flat into your left.
  Man ends up facing diagonal to the wall.
- Cross your left foot in front of your right standing on the toes with your back diagonal to the wall – slide your toes across the floor.

Forward (backward) change steps

A change step should always be performed on counts 4, 5, 6 – so only complete half a natural or reverse turn, and after the third step execute the following three count change steps:

1

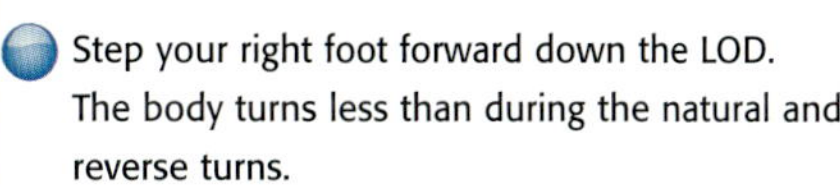

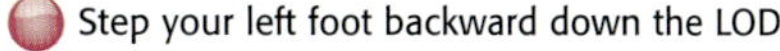

- Step your right foot forward down the LOD.
  The body turns less than during the natural and reverse turns.
- Step your left foot backward down the LOD.

2

- Now step your left foot diagonal to the center – toe leads.
- Step your right foot backward diagonally backing to the wall.

3

- Close your right foot to your left, sliding the flat of your right foot to meet your left.
  Man ends facing diagonal to the wall, preparing to take the first step of his reverse turn down the LOD with his left foot.
- Close your left foot to your right, sliding the flat of your left foot to meet your right.
  Lady ends up backing diagonal to the wall, preparing to take the first step of her reverse turn down the LOD with her right foot.

Change steps: More experienced dancers often use the backward change step as well as the forward change step. This simply involves the man copying exactly what the lady does on the forward change steps, and the lady performing the man's forward change steps. Just swap parts, reversing the shown steps!

The Foxtrot

The Foxtrot has its roots in vaudeville. Californian actor Arthur Carringford (1882-1959), who adopted the stage name of Harry Fox, incorporated a comic walk to ragtime music into his act, and this became known as 'Fox's Trot.' Harry famously worked with (and married) Yansci Dolly of the Dolly Sisters, and in 1914, both he and Yansci – later known as Jennie – were appearing at the New York Theater, then undergoing conversion into a movie palace.

Harry's vaudeville act there was scheduled between film showings – and having seen his 'Fox's Trot,' audiences flocked upstairs to the theater's roof, which had been refashioned as a *Jardin de danse*, to perform it themselves. His show won plaudits from *Variety* magazine, which commented, in May 1914: 'The debut of Harry Fox as a lone star and act amidst the films…at the New York Theater started off with every mark of success.' It added that 'the Dolly Sisters are dancing nightly on the New York Roof, [where] gold cups will be given away next week to the winners of dance contests.'

After Harry Fox had launched the Foxtrot, the talented and dynamic husband-and-wife dance team Vernon and Irene Castle gave the dance its signature grace and style. The Foxtrot went on to evolve into the combined mixture of slow and quick steps danced today – a formulation that allows for greater flexibility and variety than any other ballroom dance.

Above and opposite: The Foxtrot is an extremely versatile dance which can be performed to a variety of musical styles and tempos.

Foxtrot Facts

• **noun** a ballroom dance having an uneven rhythm with the alternation of slow and quick steps.

• **verb** (foxtrotted, foxtrotting) dance the Foxtrot.

Mood: jazzy, smoky, carefree, American, Frank Sinatra

Time: 4/4

Basic count: slow, slow, quick, quick

Beats per bar: 4

Tempo: 28–32 bars per minute

Hold position: Ballroom hold

Suggested track: *It Had To Be You* by Harry Connick, Jr.

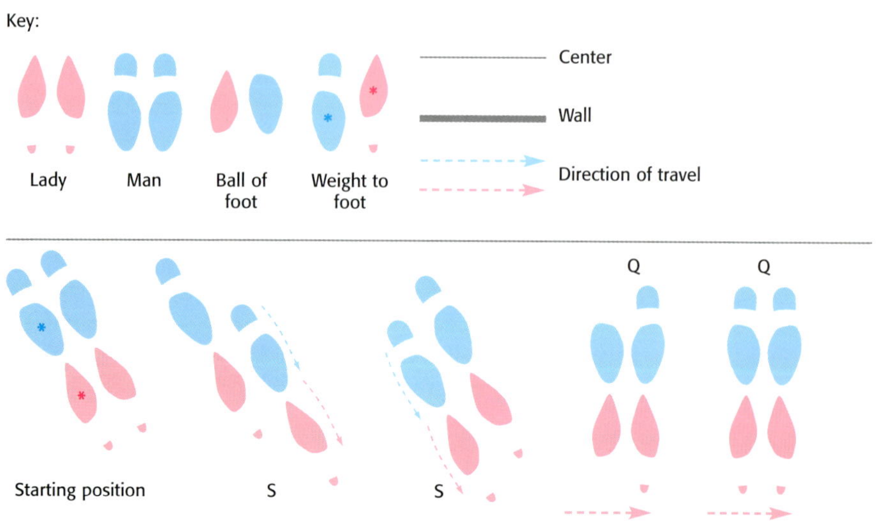

Social or Rhythm Foxtrot Steps – 1

The Social Foxtrot is ideal for beginners: it's one of the easiest ballroom dances to learn, as well as being one of the most flexible and enjoyable. It's based on a natural walking action, and can be danced to a wide range of music – from 1940s and '50s favorites to more modern 4/4 timed numbers. Mastering the simple series of steps shown below should provide you with the confidence you need to get onto the dance floor and perform the Social Foxtrot at weddings and other festive occasions.

Before you begin

Use the classic Ballroom Hold for the Social Foxtrot (see *Dance Holds* on pages 18-19). All of the walks in the Social Foxtrot, except those used when you perform the Promenade, are heel lead when walking forward and toe lead walking backward. The side taps featured in this dance are ball-flat followed by a ball-tap (see explanations on pages 16-17).

Basic

Suggested choreography: Try two of these basic steps – one facing diagonally to the outside wall (outside of the room), and one set facing diagonally to the center of the room.

- Man begins facing diagonal to the outside wall. Weight should be in the right foot, ready to move off with the left.
- Lady begins backing diagonal to the outside wall. Weight should be in the left foot, ready to move off with the right.

1

Slow

- Walk forward on your left foot, facing diagonal to the wall.
- Walk backward on your right foot, backing diagonal to the wall.

2

Slow

- Walk forward on your right foot, facing diagonal to the wall.
- Walk backward on your left foot, backing diagonal to the wall.

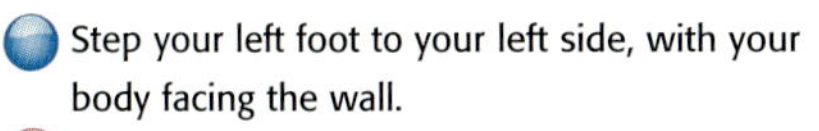

Step your left foot to your left side, with your body facing the wall.

Step your right foot to your right side, facing the center.

Close your right foot to your left foot, still facing the wall.

Close your left foot to your right foot, still facing the center.

Walk backward on your left foot, backing diagonal center.

Walk forward on your right foot, toward diagonal center.

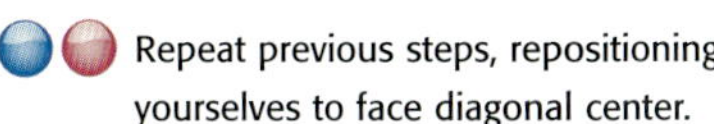

Repeat previous steps, repositioning yourselves to face diagonal center.

Walk backward on your right foot, moving toward diagonal center.

Walk forward on your left foot, moving toward diagonal center.

The man now repeats the side steps facing toward the wall, and the lady repeats the side steps facing toward the center.

Step your left foot to your left side, with your body facing the wall.

Step your right foot to your right side, facing the center.

Close your right foot to your left foot, still facing the wall.

Close your left foot to your right foot, while continuing to face the center.

Social or Rhythm Foxtrot Steps – 2

Side taps

All the man's side steps are performed facing toward the wall. All the lady's side steps are performed facing toward the center.

Suggested choreography: Dance four of these side taps in a row, traveling sideways along the line of dance.

1

Quick

- Step your left foot to your left side, while facing toward the wall.
- Step your right foot to your right side, facing the center.

2

- Ball-tap your right foot to your left, still facing the wall.
- Ball-tap your left foot to your right, still facing the center.

3

- Step your right foot to your right side.
- Step your left foot to your left side.

4

- Ball-tap your left foot to your right, still facing the wall.
- Ball-tap your right foot to your left, still facing the wall.

5

- Step your left foot to your left side (ball-flat).
- Step your right foot to your right side (ball-flat).

6

Quick

- Close your right foot to your left foot (ball-flat), still facing the wall.
- Close your left foot to your right foot (ball-flat), still facing the center.

Promenades

Before commencing the promenade, the man must adjust his hold slightly (right) by opening his right forearm from the elbow in order to allow the lady to face toward diagonal center.

When promenading, the lady will be directed by the man to face diagonal center with her body. This will enable her to step forward and across on her left foot.

See Dance Holds on pages 18-19 for more information about promenades and other holds.

Suggested choreography: Try dancing four of these promenades in a row down the line of dance (i.e. in the direction you are traveling.) The side taps are all danced on the Quick count – so if you dance them four times, you'll use up 24 counts.

1

Slow

- Step your left foot forward down the line of dance, with heel leading and toes facing diagonal to the wall.
- Step your right foot forward down the line of dance, with heel leading and toes facing diagonal to the center.

2

Slow

- Step your right foot across in front of your left, again down the line of dance.
- Step your left foot across in front of your right, again down the line of dance.

3

Quick

- Step your left foot to your left side (ball-flat step) now facing the wall.
- Step your right foot to your right side (ball-flat step) now facing the center of the room.

4

Quick

- Close your right foot to your left (ball-flat step), still facing the wall.
- Close your left foot to your right (ball-flat step), still facing the center.

The Tango

The Tango evokes strong images of passionate couples in steamy bars and on the back streets of Buenos Aires. Nonetheless, the baille con corte *or 'dance with a stop' originated in Spain and Morocco. During the 1890s, it became popular with the Argentinian lower classes, and was particularly associated with 'ladies of the night,' who would perform it solo to attract business.*

Gradually the Tango spread across the world, becoming less erotically overt – and, consequently, acceptable to a much wider range of dancers and audiences. Over time, it has changed further, with its rhythms acquiring a more *staccato* (detached) quality; although the characteristic close hold and intertwined movements remain. Tango is a walking dance: in contrast to other ballroom styles, the feet do not skim across the floor, but are lifted and placed deliberately. Its direction curves slightly to the left: this developed as a result of dancing on small floors in bars, where the participants would have had to maneuver round the tables.

The Ballroom Tango is danced in a tight, rigid ballroom hold. By contrast, the moves for the Argentine Tango are less formal, emphasizing expressiveness, intimacy, and passion in performance. Needless to say, however, the Ballroom Tango still requires strong aggression and sensuality! The steps themselves are relatively easy to learn: however, feel and mood are the essential factors.

Above and opposite: The Tango's hold and style are said to have originated among the gauchos of Argentina, who wore leather chaps that would harden from the foam and sweat of their hard-ridden horses. As a result, the gauchos walked with their knees flexed. After a long day in the saddle, they would go to bars, and ask the girls to dance. In those days the lady would dance in the crook of the cowboy's right arm, holding her head back to avoid the smell of his sweat. Her right hand was held low on the man's left hip, close to his pocket, searching for money in return for dancing with him.

Tango Facts

• **noun** (pl. tangos) **1** a ballroom dance that evolved in Buenos Aires, characterized by marked rhythms and postures and abrupt pauses. **2** a piece of music in the style of this dance.

• **verb** (tangoes, tangoed) dance the Tango.

Mood: passion, red, black, Argentina, love

Time: 2/4

Basic count: slow, slow, quick, quick, slow

Beats per bar: 2

Tempo: 30–33 bars per minute

Hold position: Tango hold

Suggested track: *Roxanne* by The Police

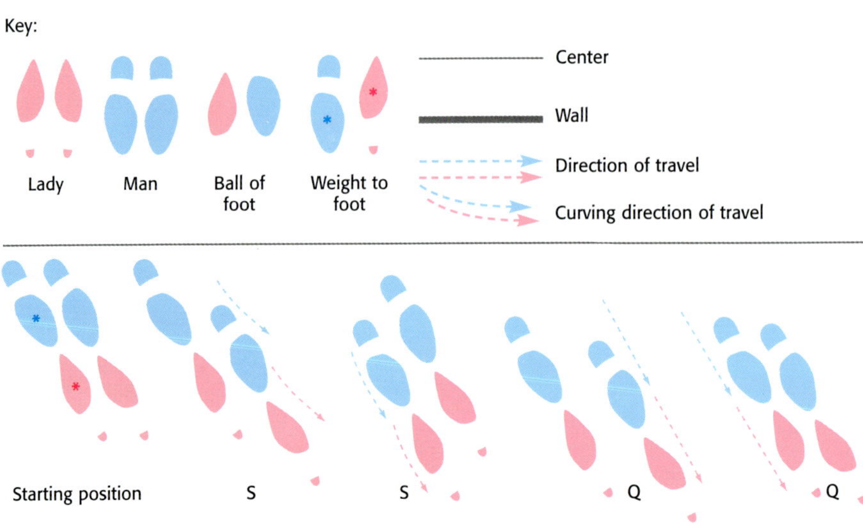

Tango Steps – 1

There are some distinct technical differences when performing the Tango in comparison with the other dances in the Ballroom section. The main disparities are:

The hold: the man adopts the Tango hold – see pages 18-19.
The right foot always closes in just behind the left (see picture right).
The floor pattern: Tango steps curve slightly whilst traveling forward; this will be described as a heel lead walk, curving slightly toward the LOD. The traveling motion of the Tango is often characterized as a 'crab-like' movement.

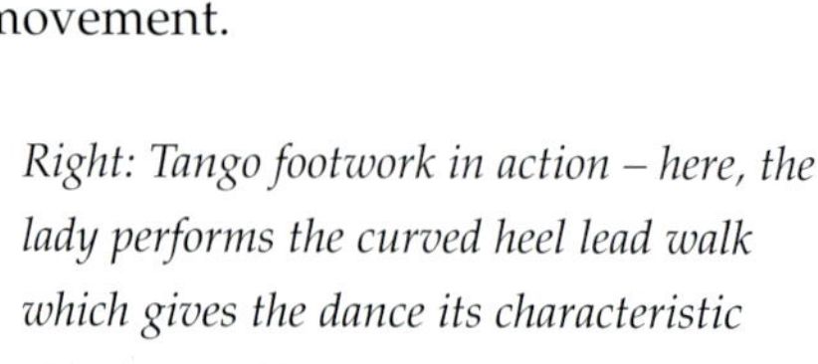

Right: Tango footwork in action – here, the lady performs the curved heel lead walk which gives the dance its characteristic sideways motion.

Tango walks

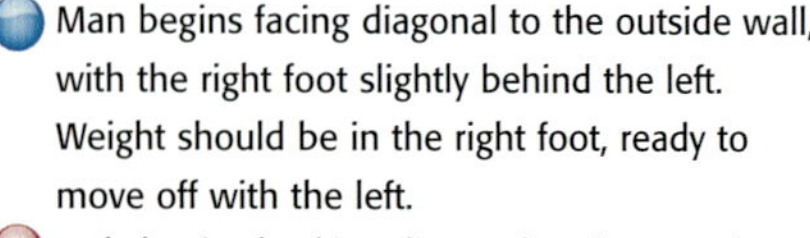

- Man begins facing diagonal to the outside wall, with the right foot slightly behind the left. Weight should be in the right foot, ready to move off with the left.
- Lady begins backing diagonal to the outside wall. Weight should be in the left, ready to move off with the right.

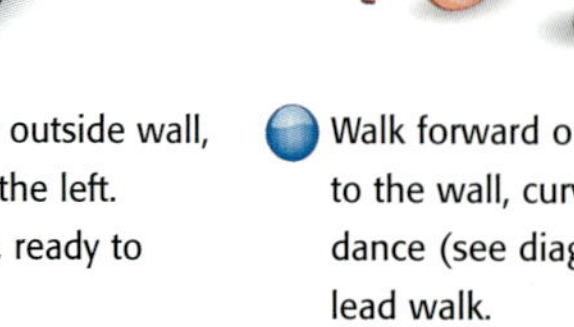

- Walk forward on your left foot, facing diagonal to the wall, curving slightly toward the line of dance (see diagram of feet on page 40). Heel lead walk.
- Walk straight back on your right foot, backing diagonal to the wall, toe lead walk.

- Walk forward on your right foot, facing diagonal to the wall, curving slightly toward the line of dance. Heel lead walk.
- Walk straight back on your left foot, backing diagonal to the wall, toe lead walk.

Two progressive side steps

- Step forward on your left foot.
- Step back on your right foot.

- Place your right foot almost to your left foot, nearly closing, still facing the wall. As you close your right foot, place it just behind your left, on the flat of the foot, just wider than your starting position.
- Close your left foot to your right foot, still backing the wall. As you close your left foot, place it just behind your right, on the flat of the foot, just wider than your starting position.

Think of this section as being two large walks followed by two much smaller walks.

Tango rocks

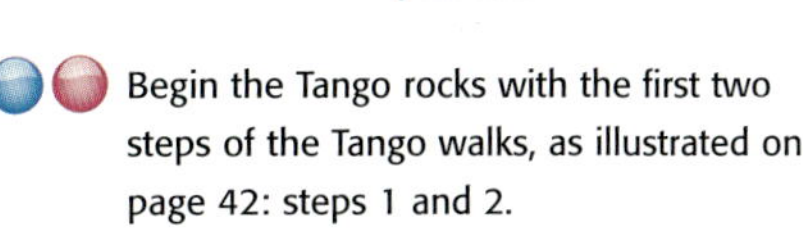

Begin the Tango rocks with the first two steps of the Tango walks, as illustrated on page 42: steps 1 and 2.

- Rock backward, transferring the weight into the left foot, releasing the toes of the right.
- Rock forward, transferring the weight into the right foot, releasing the heel of the left.

- Rock forward, transferring the weight into the right foot, releasing the heel of the left.
- Rock backward, transferring the weight into the left foot, releasing the toes of the right.

- Rock backward, transferring the weight into the left foot, releasing the toes of the right.
- Rock forward, transferring the weight into the right foot, releasing the heel of the left.

Tango Steps – 2

Corté

1

Quick

- Walk backward on your right foot, toward the center.
- Step forward on your left foot, facing diagonal center.

2

Quick

- Step your left foot to your left side, body facing the wall, but with the toes of your left foot pointing diagonal to the wall.
- Step your right foot to your right side, backing the wall, but with the toes of your right foot pointing diagonal to the center.

3

Slow

- Close your right foot to your left foot, placing it slightly behind your left, ending up facing diagonal to the center (just wider than your starting position).
- Close your left foot to your right foot, placing it slightly behind your left, ending up backing diagonal to center.

- Man and lady now perform two tango walks (see preceding pages).

Basic reverse turn

Facing diagonal to center:

- Step forward on your left foot, heel lead.
- Step your right foot backward, toe lead.

- Right foot steps to the side, toe lead, backing wall at this point.
- Step your left foot to the left side as shown in the photograph, with your body facing diagonal to the wall.

Cross your left foot in front of your right, standing on the flat.

Close your right foot to the left, facing the LOD.

The heel releases naturally in Tango walks and rocks.

Right foot steps back down the line of dance.

Left foot steps forward along the line of dance.

Step your left foot to your left side, body facing the wall, but with the toes of your left foot pointing diagonal to the wall.

Step your right foot sideways, toe lead (slightly behind the left foot), body facing center.

Close your right foot to your left foot, your right foot just behind your left on the flat of the foot (just wider than your starting position). You're now ready to recommence the sequence of steps, following the suggested choreography.

Close your left foot to your right foot, your right foot just behind your left on the flat of the foot (just wider than your starting position). You're now ready to recommence the sequence of steps, following the suggested choreography.

Suggested choreography: Try performing two sets of Tango walks, one set of the Tango rocks, two Tango walks, and the basic reverse turn.

The Quickstep

The Quickstep developed in the post-World War I era, from Harry Fox's Foxtrot – a slower dance whose fame had previously spread rapidly on both sides of the Atlantic following its adoption by the husband-and-wife team of Vernon and Irene Castle. The Castles' other innovations included the 'Castle Walk:' described as 'sliding and poetical' by the couple themselves, this could be danced in either quick or slow tempo, and has direct associations with modern Foxtrot and Quickstep styles.

The Quickstep, which is also closely linked with another American dance craze, the Charleston, achieved mass popularity in the 1920s, and was performed to the swinging Big Band tunes of the period. Ideally suited to the fast pace of these numbers, it offers today's dancers an energetic and exhilarating workout that is as pleasing to the feet as it is beneficial to the cardiovascular system!

Left: Dancers Irene and Vernon Castle. In 1939, a movie of their life story appeared, starring Fred Astaire and Ginger Rogers. Right and opposite: The Quickstep is one of the most invigorating of all Ballroom dances.

Quickstep Facts

- **noun** a fast foxtrot in 4/4 time.

Mood: lively, Charleston, English, elegant, fast, happy

Time: 4/4

Basic count: slow, slow, quick, quick, slow

Beats per bar: 4

Tempo: 48–50 bars per minute

Hold position: standard ballroom hold

Suggested track: *Monsters Inc.* by Randy Newman

Key:

Lady

Man

Ball of foot

Weight to foot

Center

Wall

Direction of travel

Curving direction of travel

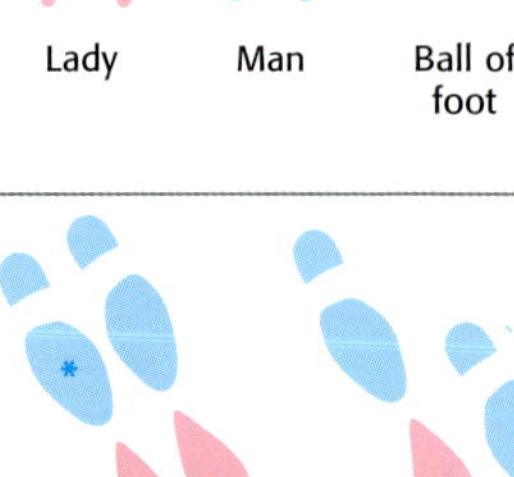

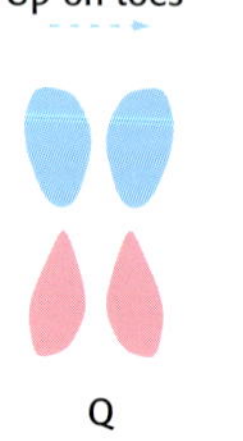

Quickstep Steps – 1

The following suggested choreography for the Quickstep incorporates the outside partner position, which in this instance is initiated by the man. Ladies needn't concern themselves with it too much, as the man will lead them into this position.

Quarter-turn to the right

1

- Man begins facing diagonal to the outside wall. Weight should be in the right foot, ready to move off with the left.
- Lady begins backing diagonal to the outside wall. Weight should be in the left foot, ready to move off with the right.

Opposite top: Dancing the Quickstep demands poise and elegance as well as agility.

2

Slow

- Walk forward on your left foot, facing diagonal to the wall – this should be executed as a natural walking movement.
- Walk straight back on your right foot, backing diagonal to the wall.

Reflections on dance

'You don't stop dancing from growing old, you grow old because you stop dancing.'

Anon

3

Slow

- Walk forward on your right foot, facing diagonal to the wall.
- Walk straight back on your left foot, backing diagonal to the wall.

- Chassé: step your left foot to your left side, facing the wall.
- Chassé: step your right foot to your right side, facing the center.

- Close your right foot to your left foot on your toes, still facing the wall. As you do this, allow your body to turn slightly to the left.
- Close your left foot to your right foot on your toes. As you do so, allow your body to turn slightly to the right.

- Step your left foot to your left side and slightly back – ending up with your body backing diagonal to the center.
- Step your right foot to your right side and slightly forward – ending up facing diagonal to the center.

Quickstep Steps – 2

Progressive chassé

- Walk backward on your right foot, backing diagonal toward center.
- Step forward on your left foot, with your body facing diagonal center.

- Step your left foot to your left side facing the wall, but with the toes of your left foot pointing diagonal to the wall.
- Step your right foot to your right side backing the wall, but with the toes of your right foot pointing diagonal to the center.

- Close your right foot to your left on your toes, ending up facing diagonal to the wall.
- Close your left foot to your right foot on your toes, ending up backing diagonal to the wall.

- Left foot steps to the side and slightly forward on your toes.
- Right foot steps to the side and slightly back on your toes.

Lock step

- Step your right foot forward, heel lead, facing diagonal to the wall in an outside partner position. Allow the left shoulder to move slightly toward the right foot.
- Step your left foot backward, toe lead, backing diagonal to the wall. Allow the right shoulder to move slightly toward the left foot.

- Step the left foot forward and slightly to the side on your toes.
- Step back on your right foot, toe lead.

- Right foot crosses behind the left on the toes.
- Left foot crosses in front of the right foot: you may allow the toe of the left foot to release when moving into the crossed position.

Left: The dancers should appear to be light on their feet while performing the Quickstep.

Suggested choreography: Begin by trying one quarter-turn to the right followed by a progressive chassé and the lock step. This sequence can then be repeated as many times as required.

- Step your left foot forward and slightly to the side, ending up facing diagonal to the wall. This leads into the first step of the quarter-turn to the right, still in an outside partner position.
- Step your right foot backward and slightly to the side, still backing diagonal to the wall. This leads into the first step of the quarter-turn to the right.

Latin American Dances

Typically, the Samba, Rumba, Cha Cha and Paso Doble are the four dances classified as 'Latin American' – even though the Paso Doble originated in Spain, not in South America. Another surprise is the omission of the Tango from this category: while its roots are Argentinian (see pages 40-41), Ballroom Tango is invariably placed in the Ballroom International Standard grouping at competition level. Salsa, although not judged in the Latin American section, is an increasingly popular dance throughout the world, competed in its own right.

In Latin American dance contests, ladies wear colorful, short, fringed and often beaded skirts, and men appear in tight-fitting pants and tops. These outfits – reminiscent of the extravagant and flamboyant costumes worn in carnival processions at Mardi Gras – accentuate the performers' leg lines, and bring attention to the rhythmic hip movements that characterize the dances in this section.

Latin American Overview

Latin American dance, and the music that inspires it, are the fruits of a remarkable cultural cross-fertilization between African and European influences – forged over hundreds of years of slavery in South America and the Caribbean, adapted to satisfy the tastes and circumstances of subsequent generations, and introduced to eager new audiences and would-be performers in North American and European clubs and ballrooms during the early decades of the 20th century.

The USA's love affair with all things Latin, initially boosted by a groundswell of immigration from countries like Puerto Rico – which became a territory of the United States as a result of the 'Jones Act' of 1917 – and Cuba, was further fanned, in the 1930s and '40s, by what Sue Steward's recent history of Salsa has described as 'a spate of Hollywood kitsch musicals featuring exotic song-and-dance intervals.' Such movies did well in Europe, too: but Latin music and dance, though firmly established in Paris by the 1920s, were a little slower to achieve widespread popularity in Britain. According to Frank Borrows (whose book on the *Theory and Technique of Latin American Dancing*, published in 1948, was the earliest detailed guide to the subject to appear in the UK), it was the Rumba that really caught the imagination of British dancers – thanks, in part, to an influential demonstration of its steps by a French couple, the Chapouls, at London's fashionable Café de Paris in 1932.

After World War II, these and other once unfamiliar Latin American dances were quickly adopted by dance 'officialdom' on both sides of the Atlantic, with bodies such as the National Association of Teachers of Dancing and the International Dancing Masters Association incorporating them into their examination syllabuses, and a steadily growing number of competitions springing up to showcase them. Since then, a succession of star Latin dancers has emerged, and it's a sign of the genre's truly international status that one of its most highly rated current performers is Maksim Chmerkovskiy, a Russian now based in the USA!

Above: Latin American dance star Maksim Chmerkovskiy.
Right and opposite: The Salsa and Samba are designed to thrill!

The Rumba

The Rumba is widely thought of as the signature dance of Cuba – although many other popular Latin dances have originated in that island. Their roots lie in the dances, instruments, and rhythms that African slaves first brought to the Caribbean in the 16th century. This music and culture mingled, over generations, with that of the Spaniards and other Europeans who owned land and property in the West Indies, and the result was a rich and fascinating synthesis of styles and traditions. In time, even the Waltz found its way across the Atlantic into the dance clubs and salons of Cuba!

Cuban music is layered with complex rhythms and syncopations. However, beginners should try not to focus too much on these, but concentrate on their footwork instead! The steps for the Rumba present quite a challenge for the novice; but once mastered, this romantic and sultry dance is entrancing to watch and perform.

As with many of the Latin dances, the steps repeat three or four times on alternating sides. When you see this symbol * the steps shown will be a repetition on the opposite side.

Above and opposite: The Rumba's sultry mood has a perennial appeal for dancers.

Rumba Facts

Rumba or **Rhumba**

• **noun 1** a rhythmic dance with Spanish and African elements, originating in Cuba. **2** a ballroom dance based on this.

• **verb** (rumbaed or rumba'd, rumbaing) dance the Rumba.

Mood: slow, sensual, romantic, hot, Cuba

Time: 4/4

Basic count: slow, quick, quick

Beats per bar: 4

Tempo: 26-32 bars per minute

Hold position: open hold

Suggested track: *The Girl from Ipanema* by Frank Sinatra

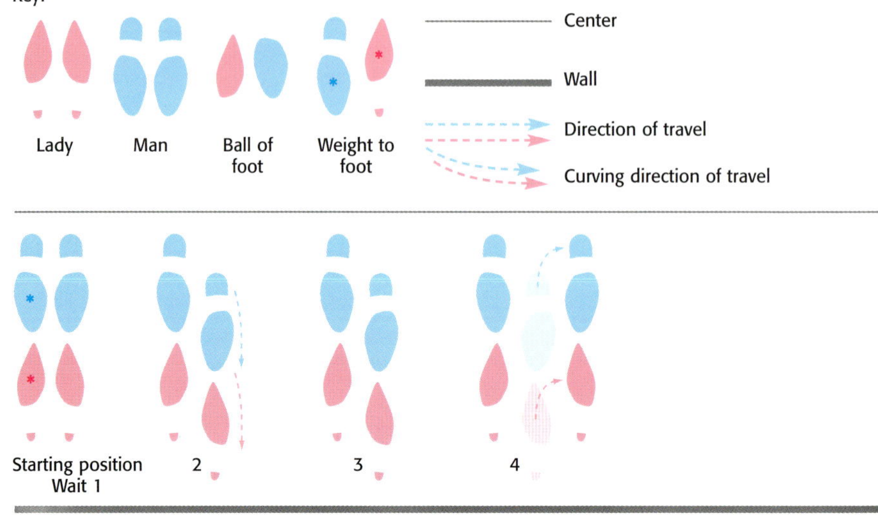

Rumba Steps – 1

The Rumba is among the slowest and most seductive and sensual of Latin dances. This sensuality is achieved by maintaining close contact with the floor through the feet; imagine they're having an affair with its surface! As one foot passes the other, try to keep the toes of the moving leg in contact with the floor.

When transferring your weight in the Rumba, you must straighten the knee of the new standing leg just before taking weight onto it. Immediately after this, settle your weight onto the hip of the standing leg, as you would when standing at a bus stop or carrying a child on your hip. (See Footwork section on pages 16-17 for further details.) Settling the weight over the new standing leg achieves the Latin hip action that is so familiar in this dance. When a dance step occurs on count 4, the settling action of the weight occurs on count 1 on the same leg.

1	2	3	4	1	2	3	4
Hip	Step	Step	Step	Hip	Step	Step	Step

Where a step shown begins on count 2, remember that count 1 is used for settling the weight onto the hip of the leg you are standing on in the preceding step.

Rumba basic

- Man begins facing the wall. Weight can either be in the right foot, with the left foot relaxed to the left side, or weight can be transferred onto the right foot on count 1 in preparation for count 2.
- Lady begins backing the wall. Weight can either be in the left foot, with the right foot relaxed to the right side, or weight can be transferred onto the left foot on count 1 in preparation for count 2.

1

- Wait.

Reflections on dance

'Dancing is the perpendicular expression of a horizontal desire.'

Anon

2

- Forward checked walk: step forward on the left foot, with toes pointing slightly outward.
- Back basic: step backward on the right foot, toes pointing slightly outward.

3

Transfer weight back to right foot, releasing the heel of the left foot.

Transfer weight forward to left foot, releasing the heel of the right foot.

4

Step the left foot to your left side, toes maintaining contact with the floor, tracking the foot back toward the right foot before transferring weight to the left side.

Step your right foot to your right side, toes maintaining contact with the floor, tracking the foot back toward the left foot before transferring the weight to the right side.

5

Hold/hip.

6

Step backward on your right foot, toes pointing slightly outward.

Step forward on the left foot, toes pointing slightly outward.

7

Transfer weight forward to your left foot, releasing the heel of the right foot.

Transfer weight back to your right foot, releasing the heel of the left foot.

8

Step your right foot to your right side, toes maintaining contact with the floor, tracking the foot back toward the left foot before transferring the weight to the right side.

Step the left foot to your left side, toes maintaining contact with the floor, tracking the foot back toward the right foot before transferring weight to the left side.

Rumba Steps – 2

New Yorks with a turn

Use the side-by-side Latin hold position (see pages 18-19)

New Yorks

1

- Turn against the LOD, moving the ball of the left foot past the side of the right foot...
- Turn against the LOD, moving the ball of your right foot past the side of the left foot...

2

- ...as you travel forward into a checked walk with the left foot.
- ...as you travel forward into a checked walk with the right foot.

3

- Transfer the weight back onto the right foot.
- Transfer the weight back onto the left foot.

4

- Step left foot to left side to turn back and face your partner (starting position); weight settles into the hip on count 1.
- Step right foot to right side to turn back and face your partner (starting position); weight settles into the hip on count 1.

1

- Right foot passes the left foot, with toes maintaining contact with the floor, to repeat the New York to the opposite side.
- Left foot passes the right foot, with toes in contact with the floor, to repeat the New York to the opposite side.

2*

- As you travel forward into a checked walk on the right...
- As you travel forward into a checked walk on the left...

3*

4*

...transfer the weight back to the left foot.
...transfer the weight back to the right foot.

Step right foot to right side to turn back and face your partner (starting position); weight settles into the hip on count 1.
Step left foot to left side to turn back and face your partner (starting position); weight settles into the hip on count 1.

> **Reflections on dance**
>
> *'The one thing that can solve most of our problems is dancing. Any problem in the world can be solved by dancing.'*
>
> James Brown (1933-2006)

Turn

1 Hold/hip.

2

Step forward on the right foot, turning on the left foot against the LOD...
Step forward on the left foot, turning on the right foot against the LOD...

PIVOT ...ending up with the toes of the left foot pointing down the LOD.
PIVOT ...ending up with the toes of the right foot pointing down the LOD.

3

Transfer weight forward onto the left foot.
Transfer weight forward onto the right foot.

4

Step right foot to the right side, having made a quarter-turn to face the wall and your partner.
Step left foot to the left side, having made a quarter-turn to face the center and your partner.

Rumba Steps – 3

Shoulder to shoulder

(requires outside partner position – see pages 48-49)

1 Hold/hip.
For positions see count 8, page 59.

2

Checked walk forward on the left – stepping left foot forward and across, diagonal to the wall. Release the heel of the right foot, leaving the ball of the foot on the floor.

Step right foot back, body facing diagonal to the center, facing partner hip to hip. Release the heel of the left foot, leaving the ball of the foot on the floor.

3

Transfer weight back to the right foot.

Transfer weight forward to the left foot.

4

Step the left foot to your left side to turn back and face your partner; weight settles into the left hip on count 1.

Step the right foot to the right side to turn and face your partner; weight settles into the right hip on count 1.

Reflections on dance

'There is nothing more notable in Socrates than that he found time, when he was an old man, to learn music and dancing, and thought it time well spent.'

Michel de Montaigne (1533-1592)

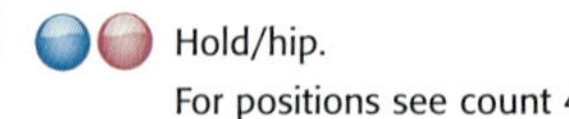

1 Hold/hip.
For positions see count 4.

2*

Checked walk forward on the right – stepping right foot forward and across, diagonal to the wall. Release the heel of the left foot, leaving the ball of the foot on the floor.

Step left foot back, body facing diagonal to the center, facing partner hip to hip. Release the heel of the right foot, leaving the ball of the foot on the floor.

Suggested choreography: Try four lots of the basic, three New Yorks, and a turn, followed by three shoulder to shoulders and an underarm turn.

The sequence of four basics runs as follows (from man's lead):

Wait 1, 2 3 4
Forward on left

Wait 1, 2 3 4
Back on right

Wait 1, 2 3 4
Forward on left

Wait 1, 2 3 4
Back on right

Transfer weight back to the left foot.
Transfer weight forward to the right foot.

Step your right foot to your right side to turn back and face your partner. Weight settles into the hip on count 1.
Step your left foot to your left side to turn back and face your partner. Weight settles into the hip on count 1.

Turn

1 Hold/hip.
For positions see count 4*.

Release the lady's left hand from your right, raising your left arm to lead her into the turn.
Release your left hand.

Step backward on your right foot, toes pointing slightly outward.
Step forward on the left foot, allowing your body to turn on the right foot to face the LOD, and ending up with the toes of the right foot pointing down the LOD.

Transfer weight forward to the left foot, releasing the heel of the left foot.
Transfer weight forward onto the right foot.

Step your right foot to your right side, toes maintaining contact with the floor, and tracking the foot back toward the left foot before transferring the weight to the right side.
Step left foot to left side, having executed a quarter-turn to face the center and your partner.

The Cha Cha

The Cha Cha (or Cha Cha Cha) became very popular in the early 1950s. It was easier to dance than its Cuban predecessor, the Mambo, and established itself quickly on the American and European social scenes, retaining its dominance there until very recently, when it was overtaken by the ever-growing Salsa craze.

Musically, the Cha Cha derives from the Mambo and another Cuban favorite, the Rumba. When the orchestras performing these two dances started to slow down their tempos, the result was the 'Triple' Mambo or 'Mambo-Rumba.' Cuban composer and violinist Enrique Jorrín (1926-1987) went on to introduce what he called the *cha-cha-chá* in about 1951, though the exact date of its origin is uncertain. Its characteristic rhythmical pattern, occurring at the end of each bar of music, can be heard as 'de de dah:' this is the triple step or 'Cha Cha Cha.' The dance is performed in an open hold, and on the spot, moving only slightly.

Right and opposite: The Cha Cha is a fun, party-time dance, particularly when performed to the rhythm of authentic Cuban music.

What's In A Name?

There are several possible derivations for the name 'Cha Cha' – it may be a verbal imitation of the slapping noise made by the sandals of dancing couples in Cuba, or an attempt to mimic the distinctive sound produced by the guiro, an instrument from Haiti widely used in Latin ensembles.

Cha Cha Facts

Cha Cha or **Cha Cha Cha**

• **noun** a ballroom dance with small steps and swaying hip movements, performed to a Latin American rhythm.

Mood: cheeky, saucy, flirtatious, Cuba

Time: 4/4

Basic count: 1, 2, 3, 4 &

Beats per bar: 4

Tempo: 28–32 bars per minute

Hold position: open hold

Suggested track: *Oye Como Va* by Santana

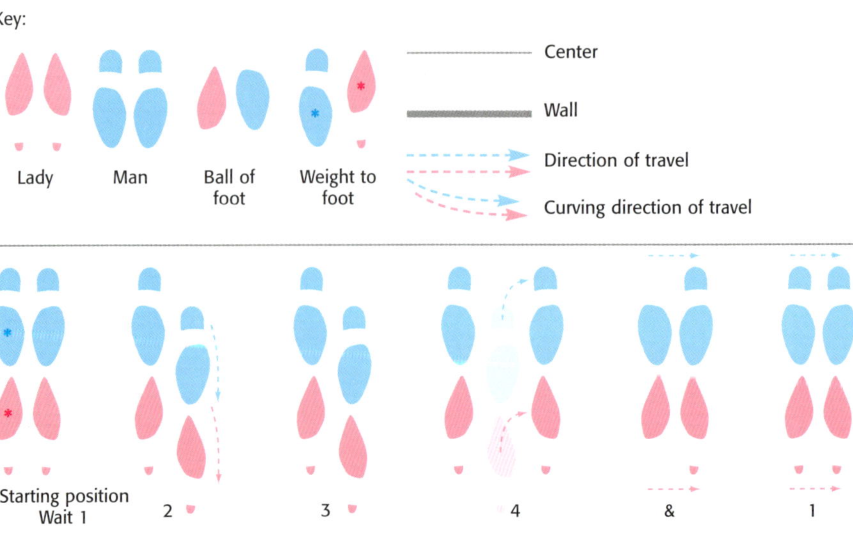

Cha Cha Steps – 1

The Cha Cha is very similar to the Rumba, but features the additional 'Cha Cha Cha chassés' at the end of every bar of four counts. These are the familiar side steps that earn the 'Cha Cha Cha' chant!

To keep things easy, and help you expand your dance repertoire quickly, the suggested choreography here is the same as for the Rumba, but with the additional chassé inserted. You should now be confident with the directions of the steps, the turns away from each other, and the lady's turn under the gentleman's arm. Once you have mastered the basic moves, try rotating slightly as you perform them, so that you are facing in different directions around the room.

Reflections on dance

'On with the dance! let joy be unconfin'd;
No sleep till morn, when youth and pleasure meet;
To chase the glowing hours with flying feet.'
Lord Byron (1788-1824) *Childe Harold's Pilgrimage*

Cha Cha basic

Man begins facing the wall. Weight can either be in the right foot, with the left foot relaxed to the left side – or may be transferred onto the right foot on count 1, in preparation for count 2.

Lady begins backing the wall. Weight can either be in the left foot, with the right foot relaxed to the right side – or may be transferred onto the left foot on count 1 in preparation for count 2. See opening of 'Rumba basic' (earlier in this chapter on pages 58-59) for a photograph of these starting positions.

1

Wait.

'Cha Cha Cha chassé' (count 4 & 1 or 'Cha Cha Cha')

2

Forward checked walk: step forward on the left foot, with toes pointing slightly outward.

Back basic: step backward on the right foot, toes pointing slightly outward.

3

Transfer weight back to right foot, releasing the heel of the left foot.

Transfer weight forward to left foot, releasing the heel of the right foot.

4

Cha

Step your left foot to your left side, toes maintaining contact with the floor, tracking the foot back toward the right foot.

Step your right foot to your right side, toes maintaining contact with the floor, tracking the foot back toward the left foot.

&

Cha

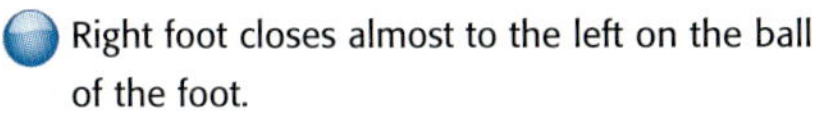

- Right foot closes almost to the left on the ball of the foot.
- Left foot closes almost to the right on the ball of the foot.

1

Cha

- Left foot takes a small step to the left side.
- Right foot takes a small step to the right side.

The 'Cha Cha Cha chassé' can easily be remembered as 'step close step' to whichever direction you are facing.

2*

- Step back on the right foot, with toes pointing slightly outward.
- Step forward on the left foot, with toes pointing slightly outward.

3*

- Transfer weight forward to the left foot, releasing the heel of the right foot.
- Transfer weight back to the right foot, releasing the heel of the left foot.

4*

- Step your right foot to the right side, toes maintaining contact with the floor, tracking the foot back toward the left foot.
- Step your left foot to the left side, toes maintaining contact with the floor, tracking the foot back toward the right foot.

&*

- Left foot closes almost to the right on the ball of the foot.
- Right foot closes almost to the left on the ball of the foot.

1*

- Right foot takes a small step to the right side.
- Left foot takes a small step to the left side.

Cha Cha Steps – 2

New Yorks with a turn

Uses the side-by-side Latin hold position (see pages 18-19)

New Yorks

- Turn against the LOD, moving the ball of the left foot past the side of the right foot...
- Turn against the LOD, moving the ball of your right foot past the side of the left foot...

- ...as you travel forward into a checked walk with the left foot facing the LOD.
- ...as you travel forward into a checked walk with the right foot facing the LOD.

- Transfer the weight back onto the right foot.
- Transfer the weight back onto the left foot.

'Cha Cha Cha chassé' (count 4 & 1 or 'Cha Cha Cha')

- Step left foot to left side to turn back and face your partner (starting position).
- Step right foot to right side to turn back and face your partner (starting position).

- Right foot closes almost to the left on the ball of the foot.
- Left foot closes almost to the right on the ball of the foot.

- Left foot takes a small step to the left side.
- Right foot takes a small step to the right side.

- Turn toward the LOD, moving the ball of the right foot past the side of the left foot.
- Turn toward the LOD, moving the ball of your left foot past the side of the right foot.

Right foot passes the left foot, toes maintaining contact with the floor, to repeat the New York to the opposite side.

Left foot passes the right foot, toes in contact with the floor, to repeat the New York to the opposite side.

Repeat these steps to the opposite side, as shown below.

Transfer the weight back onto the left foot.

Transfer the weight back onto the right foot.

Reflections on dance

'There is a bit of insanity in dancing that does everybody a great deal of good.'

Edwin Denby (1903-1983)

Above: Master the Cha Cha steps and you'll be free to go wherever the rhythm takes you!

'Cha Cha Cha chassé' (count 4 & 1 or 'Cha Cha Cha')

Step right foot to the right side to turn back and face your partner (starting position).

Step left foot to the left side to turn back and face your partner (starting position).

Left foot closes almost to the right on ball of the foot.

Right foot closes almost to the left on ball of the foot.

Right foot takes a small step to the right side.

Left foot takes a small step to the left side.

Man and lady now repeat the asterisked steps above, then continue as follows:

Turn

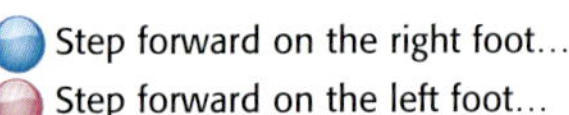

Step forward on the right foot…
Step forward on the left foot…

…turning on the left foot to face the LOD, PIVOT ending up with the toes of the left foot pointing down the LOD.
…turning on the right foot to face the LOD, PIVOT ending up with the toes of the right foot pointing down the LOD.

Transfer weight forward onto the left foot.
Transfer weight forward onto the right foot.

'Cha Cha Cha chassé' (count 4 & 1 or 'Cha Cha Cha')

Step right foot to the right side, having made a quarter-turn to face the wall – and your partner.
Step left foot to the left side, having made a quarter-turn that leaves you facing the center and your partner.

Left foot closes almost to the right on the ball of the foot.
Right foot closes almost to the left on the ball of the foot.

Right foot takes a small step to the right side.
Left foot takes a small step to the left side.

Cha Cha Steps – 3

Shoulder to shoulder and underarm turn (part one)

(requires outside partner position – see pages 48-49)

1

 Hold/hip.

2

Checked walk forward on the left – stepping, left foot forward, diagonal to the wall. Release the heel of the right foot, leaving the ball of the foot on the floor.

Step right foot back, body facing diagonal to the center, facing partner hip to hip. Release the heel of the left foot, leaving the ball of the foot on the floor.

3

Transfer weight back to the right foot.

Transfer weight forward to the left foot.

4

Cha

Cha Cha Cha chassé to the left.

Cha Cha Cha chassé to the right.

&

Cha

1

Cha

- Repeat on the right and the left, as detailed below, always stepping forward toward your partner, but in a side beside position, holding both her hands and turning diagonally toward her – shoulder to shoulder!
- Repeat on left and right, as detailed below.

- Checked walk forward on right – stepping, right foot forward, diagonal to wall.
- Step left foot back, body facing diagonal to center, facing partner hip to hip.

- Transfer weight back to the left foot.
- Transfer weight forward to the right foot.

Reflections on dance

'We're fools whether we dance or not, so we might as well dance.'

Japanese proverb

- Step right foot to the right side.
- Step left foot to the left side.

Cha

Cha Cha Steps – 4

Shoulder to shoulder and underarm turn (part two)

Suggested Choreography: Try four lots of the basic, three New Yorks, and a turn, followed by three shoulder to shoulders and an underarm turn.

The sequence of four basics runs as follows (from man's lead):

2 3 4 & 1
Forward on left

2 3 4 & 1
Back on right

2 3 4 & 1
Forward on left

2 3 4 & 1
Back on right

- Step backward on your right foot, toes pointing slightly outward. Releasing your right hand, then raise your left arm in order to lead the lady into the turn.
- Step forward on the left foot.

- Transfer weight forward onto the left foot, releasing the heel of the right foot.
- Transfer weight forward onto the right foot, turning on the left foot to face the LOD, and ending up with the toes of the right foot pointing down the LOD.

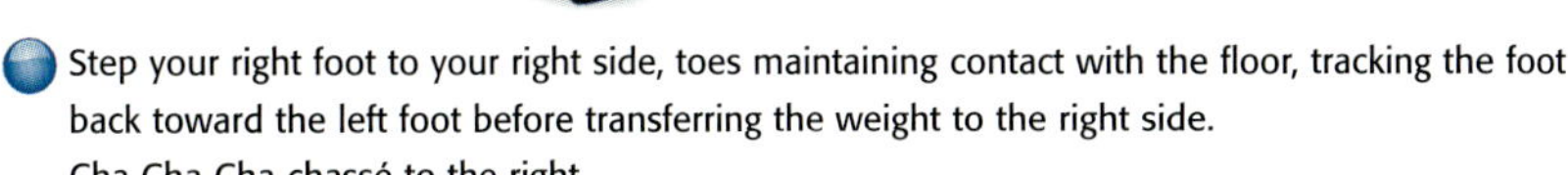

- Step your right foot to your right side, toes maintaining contact with the floor, tracking the foot back toward the left foot before transferring the weight to the right side.
  Cha Cha Cha chassé to the right.
- Step left foot to the left side, having made a quarter-turn to face the center and your partner.
  Cha Cha Cha chassé to the left.

The Samba

Because slavery was not abolished in Brazil until 1888, dancing in that country retained, for much longer than in other places, a special importance as one of the few channels of free expression available to slave communities. The tribal traditions of Dahomey, Angola, Congo, Nigeria, Guinea, and Mozambique had migrated with the slaves, who brought African dances such as the Semba and Batuque to Brazil. The name 'semba' derives from a Bantu word meaning to pray; blended with Portuguese and Amerindian dances, it became the 'Samba' that is danced today.

Thanks to its eclectic cultural heritage, Brazil has become the carnival capital of the world. Rio de Janeiro's Mardi Gras celebrations are unrivaled for the glamor and color of the costumes worn by participants. As part of the processions, the 'escolas de samba' or 'samba schools' compete rather like the bands of rival, baton-twirling majorettes that are so familiar in the USA. Each year, the samba schools rehearse intensively in order to impress the judges who watch them as they pass the specially constructed Sambadrome in downtown Rio.

The Samba was introduced to Europe in 1905, and achieved an extensive following among audiences and dancers thanks to movies such as *Flying Down to Rio* (1933), starring Fred Astaire and Ginger Rogers, and to the impact of Carmen Miranda (1909-1955), the 'Brazilian Bombshell' famed for being 'the lady in the tutti frutti hat.'

Right and opposite: Samba costumes are designed for visual impact.

Samba Facts

• **noun** a Brazilian dance of African origin.
• **verb** (sambaed or samba'd, sambaing) dance the Samba.

Mood: sexy, explosive, carnival, Carmen Miranda, Brazil
Time: 2/4
Basic count: 1, 2, 1, 2 1, 2
Beats per bar: 4
Tempo: 48–50 bars per minute
Hold position: open hold
Suggested track: *Samba Dees Days* by Charlie Byrd & Stan Getz

Key:

Lady | Man | Ball of foot | Weight to foot

Center
Wall
Direction of travel
Curving direction of travel

Starting position | 1 | Tap & | 2 | & Tap

Samba Steps – 1

The basic Samba step shown here is the very rudimentary one – enabling you to get a feel of the rhythm and motion in order to dance! The progression has also been included in brief for you to try; if you go on to attend classes or club dances, you will be able to explore it further. Enjoy the Samba…it is the essence of fun and exotic carnival feeling!

- Man begins facing the wall. Weight can either be in the right foot, with the left foot relaxed to the left side, or weight can be transferred onto the right foot on count 1 in preparation for count 2.
- Lady begins backing the wall. Weight can either be in the left foot, with the right foot relaxed to the right side, or weight can be transferred onto the left foot on count 1 in preparation for count 2.

Samba basic

1

- Step forward on the left foot.
- Small step back on your right foot.

&

- Tap the right foot next to the left foot.
- Tap the left foot next to the right foot.

2

- Step back on the right foot.
- Step forward on the left foot.

&

- Tap the left foot next to the right foot.
- Tap the right foot next to the left foot.

The more advanced basic move is similar to the Cha Cha; add two extra steps after the step forward.

1

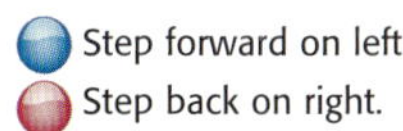

Step forward on left.
Step back on right.

&

Instead of the tap, actually briefly take weight on the right foot, releasing the left foot slightly.
Instead of the tap, actually briefly take weight on the left foot, releasing the right foot slightly.

2

Replace weight to the left foot completely.
Replace weight to the right foot completely.

Samba Steps – 2

Whisk

1

Step your left foot to your left side.
Step your right foot to your right side.

&

Cross your right foot behind your left, weight on right foot, releasing left foot slightly.
Cross your left foot behind your right, weight on left foot, releasing right foot slightly.

2

Replace weight to the left foot.
Replace weight to the right foot.

3

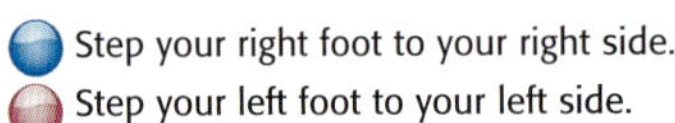

Step your right foot to your right side.

Step your left foot to your left side.

&

Cross your left foot behind your right, weight on the left foot, releasing the right foot slightly.

Cross your right foot behind your left, weight on the right foot, releasing the left foot slightly.

4

Replace weight to the right foot and return the left foot to original position.

Replace weight to the left foot and return the right foot to original position.

Samba walks in promenade and turning

&

Turn to face the LOD in a promenade position (refer to pages 18-19), but maintain a connection with your partner with your front hands, slightly facing each other to form a V-shape.

Exactly the same as the man.

1

Step forward on your left foot along the LOD.

Step forward on your right foot along the LOD.

&

Transfer weight partly back onto the right foot, pulling the left foot back slightly toward the right foot on the flat of the foot.

Transfer weight partly back onto the left foot, pulling the right foot back slightly toward the left foot on the flat of the foot.

2

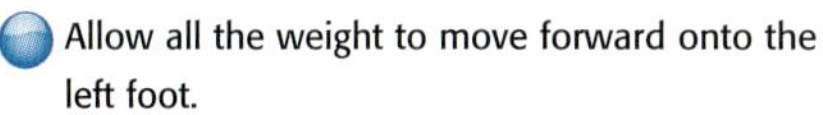

Allow all the weight to move forward onto the left foot.

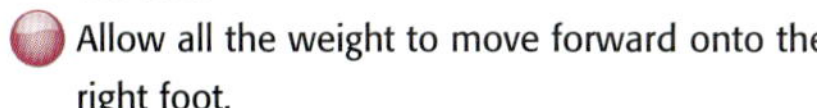

Allow all the weight to move forward onto the right foot.

3

Step forward on your right foot along the LOD.

Step forward on your left foot along the LOD.

&

Transfer weight partly back onto the left foot, pulling the right foot back slightly toward the left foot on the flat of the foot.

Transfer weight partly back onto the right foot, pulling the left foot back slightly toward the right foot on the flat of the foot.

4

Allow all the weight to move forward onto the right foot.

Allow all the weight to move forward onto the left foot.

Repeat twice more.

You can add your own arm movements at this point – try rolling your arms in front of you!

To add a nice finish to this step, turn away from your partner, and continue with four Samba walks around in a complete circle of your own – ending up facing your partner again to commence the step sequence from the beginning.

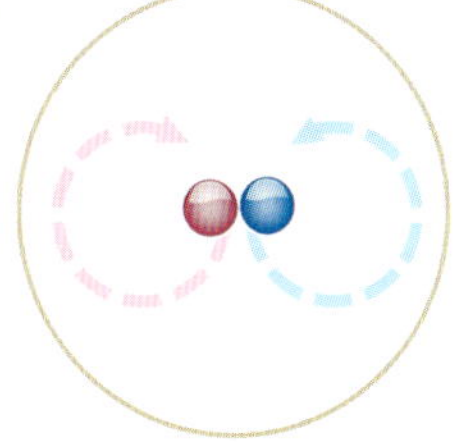

Suggested choreography: Try the basic moves four or eight times to get the feel of the music, especially if it has a fast tempo. Follow this with the Whisk step, four or eight times. Finish with the Samba walks – four in promenade position, and four to turn away from each other in your independent turns – before you begin again from the top of the Samba sequence, facing each other.

The Salsa

Salsa is a distillation of a number of Latin-American and Afro-Caribbean dances – a cocktail of rhythms and music that have mingled, over time, with jazz, rock, and even R&B and hip-hop. It is perhaps the most popular of all the Cuban-based dances, and has an ever growing worldwide following in restaurants, clubs, bars, and dance classes, where it's performed in versions for both soloists and couples.

It is hard to pinpoint exactly where the dance originated, although its mood is clearly defined by the word 'salsa' itself, which literally means 'sauce' or 'spice' in Spanish. Its steps reflect the Hispanic influences of the Dominican Republic, Colombia, Puerto Rico and Mexico among others, but it was New York City that gave it its identity…and its zesty name!

Salsa does not fall within the Latin/Standard competition category, and the many different forms it takes guarantee a fresh, spontaneous, and distinctive dance experience for its fans.

Above right and opposite: The Salsa is – quite literally – 'hot stuff'!

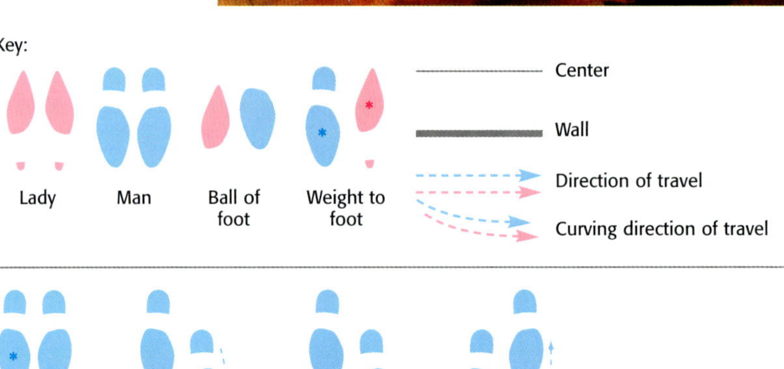

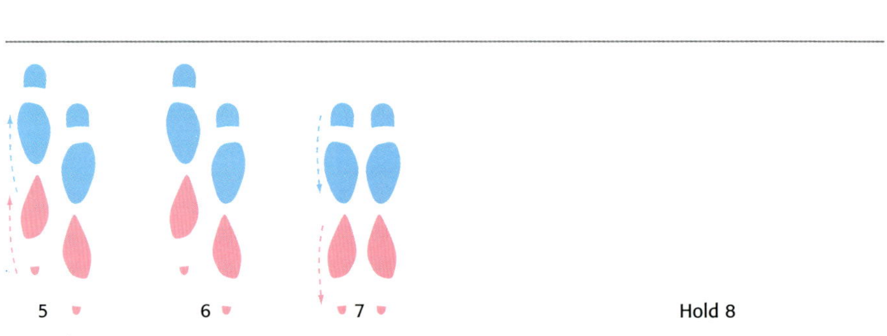

Salsa Facts

• **noun 1** a type of Latin American dance music incorporating elements of jazz and rock. **2** a dance performed to this music. **3** (especially in Latin American cookery) a spicy tomato sauce.

Mood: spicy, saucy, fun, sexy, Cuba

Time: 2/4

Basic count: quick, quick, slow

Beats per bar: 4

Tempo: 47–48 bars per minute

Hold position: open hold

Suggested track: *Mambo No. 5* by Lou Bega

Salsa Steps – 1

Salsa is taught in a variety of different ways across the world. Some perform steps on the first count, some break on 2, others break on 4. For consistency the steps shown here will commence on 1, and you will always hold on counts 4 and 8. This will give you time to settle weight into the hip, achieving that all-important, sexy, seductive look.

Salsa is also a very informal dance. Use the Latin hold featured in previous dances in this section; however, feel free to relax the position, especially if dancing on a crowded floor. This dance is fast, but intimate, so try to maintain a connection with your partner.

Throughout, use a ball-flat action with the feet (below). Keep the knees relaxed, and continue to allow the hips to move naturally as a result of what your feet and knees are doing.

Salsa basic

- Man begins facing the wall. Weight can either be in the right foot, with the left foot relaxed to the left side, or weight can be transferred onto the right foot on count 1 in preparation for count 2.
- Lady begins backing the wall. Weight can either be in the left foot, with the right foot relaxed to the right side, or weight can be transferred onto the left foot on count 1 in preparation for count 2.

1

- Step forward on the left foot, toes pointing slightly outward.
- Small step back on the right foot, toes pointing slightly outward.

2

- Replace weight back to the right foot, releasing the heel of the left foot.
- Replace weight forward to the left foot, releasing the heel of the right foot.

3

Small step back on the left foot.
Small step forward on the right foot.

4

Hold.

5

Small step back on the right foot.
Step forward on the left foot.

6

Replace weight forward to the left foot, releasing the heel of the right foot.
Replace weight back to the right foot, releasing the heel of the left foot.

7

Small step forward on the right foot.
Small step back on the left foot.

8

Hold.
As you get more confident, try to turn this step, facing different directions within the room. The man should initiate this.

Salsa Steps – 2

Back break

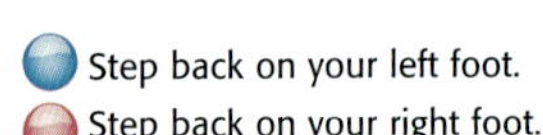
Step back on your left foot.
Step back on your right foot.

Replace weight back onto the right foot.
Replace weight back onto the left foot.

Step your left foot to meet your right foot.
Step your right foot to meet your left foot.

It may help to think 'Back, Replace, Together, Back, Replace, Together.'

4 Hold.

Step back on your right foot.
Step back on your left foot.

Replace
6

Replace weight back onto the left foot.
Replace weight back onto the right foot.

Together
7

Step your right foot to meet your left foot.
Step your left foot to meet your right foot.

8 Hold.

Side breaks

1

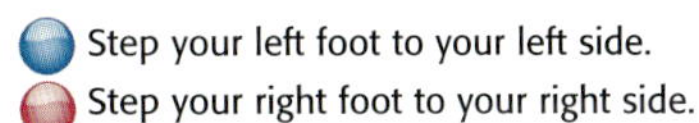

Step your left foot to your left side.
Step your right foot to your right side.

2

Replace your weight to your right foot.
Replace your weight to your left foot.

3

Step your left foot to meet your right foot.
Step your right foot to meet your left foot.

It may help to think 'Side, Side, Together, Side, Side, Together.'

4 Hold.

5

Step your right foot to your right side.
Step your left foot to your left side.

6

Replace your weight to your left foot.
Replace your weight to your right foot.

7

Step your right foot to meet your left foot.
Step your left foot to meet your right foot.

8 Hold.

Salsa Steps – 3

Basic and lady's underarm turn

1

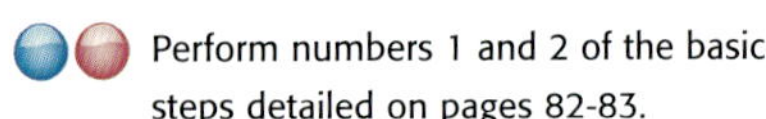

Perform numbers 1 and 2 of the basic steps detailed on pages 82-83.

2

Now continue as follows:

3

Step your left foot to the left side (as opposed to forward), raising your left arm and using your right arm to guide the lady under into the turn.

Step your right foot to your right side. Let go of the man's right arm, keeping hold with your right hand as he guides you under his raised left arm.

4 Hold.

5

Step back on your right foot, slightly crossed behind your left.

Step forward on your left foot along the LOD.

The ball of your right foot keeps contact with the floor whilst turning on the spot. This becomes imperative as you move faster.

Backing the LOD, swivel on your left foot half a turn to face the LOD, having turned under the man's arm.

6

Replace your weight to your left foot.

Step forward with your right foot.

7

Step your right foot back to meet your left, bringing both feet together.

Step your left foot to your left side, which brings you face-to-face with your partner.

Complete this sequence with a basic step forward on your left and back on your right, as shown below:

Complete this sequence with a basic step backward on your right and forward on your left, as shown below:

1

See count 1 on page 82.

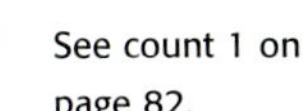

Step forward on the left foot, toes pointing slightly outward.

Small step back on the right foot, toes pointing slightly outward.

2

See count 2 on page 82.

Replace weight back to the right foot, releasing the heel of the left foot.

Replace weight forward to the left foot, releasing the heel of the right foot.

Suggested choreography: Try the basic four or eight times to get the feel of the music, especially if it has a fast tempo. Follow this by some back breaks and side breaks and complete with the underarm turn.

3

Small step back on the left foot.

Small step forward on the right foot.

4

Hold.

5

Small step back on the right foot.

Step forward on the left foot.

6

Replace weight forward to the left foot, releasing the heel of the right foot.

Replace weight back to the right foot, releasing the heel of the left foot.

7

Small step forward on the right foot.

Small step back on the left foot.

The Paso Doble

Paso Doble is Spanish for 'two step' – and the steps in question are the male dancer's bold, march-like movements, modeled on the proud, confident strutting of a matador striding into a bullring. The lady's role here is a subsidiary, though colorful and exciting one: she poses as her partner's cape!

Despite its Hispanic flavor, and the Flamenco influences that some performers bring to it, the dance actually evolved in France, where it attained widespread popularity in the years between the two World Wars. Since then, its inherent drama and passion, and the opportunities it provides for posing and display, have made it a particular favorite in Latin dance competitions. It is, however, rather less common in purely social circles – something you might seek to alter once you've mastered its intricacies!

Paso Doble Facts

• **noun** (pl. paso dobles) a fast-paced ballroom dance based on a Latin American marching style.

Mood: melodramatic, passionate, serious, Spanish

Time: 2/4

Basic count: 1, 2, 3, 4 &

Beats per bar: 2

Tempo: 60 bars per minute

Hold position: close hold

Suggested track: *Viva! Paso Doble* by the Columbia Ballroom Orchestra

Above and opposite: Boldness and flamboyance embody the essence of the Paso Doble.

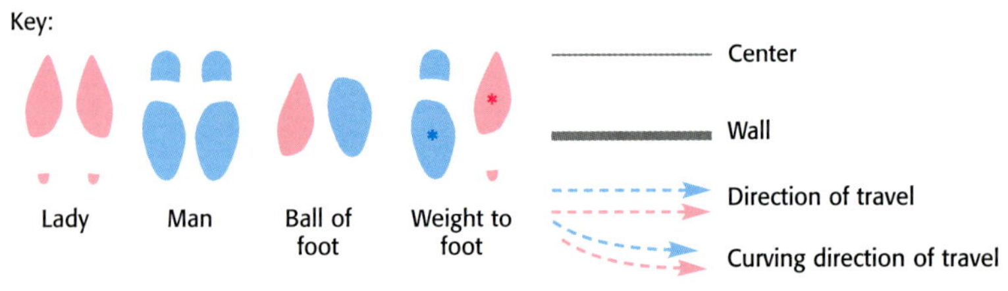

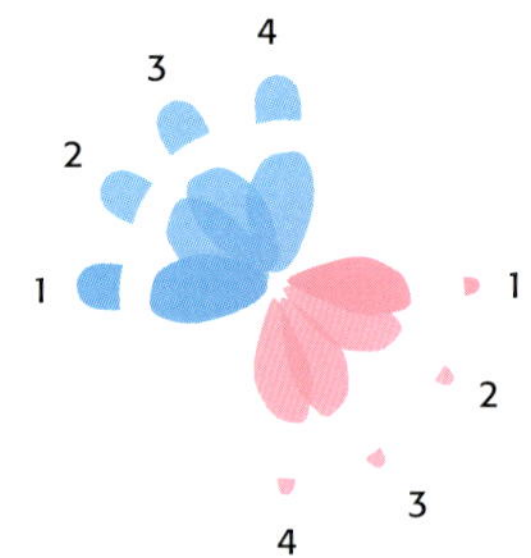

NB: These steps take place on the spot

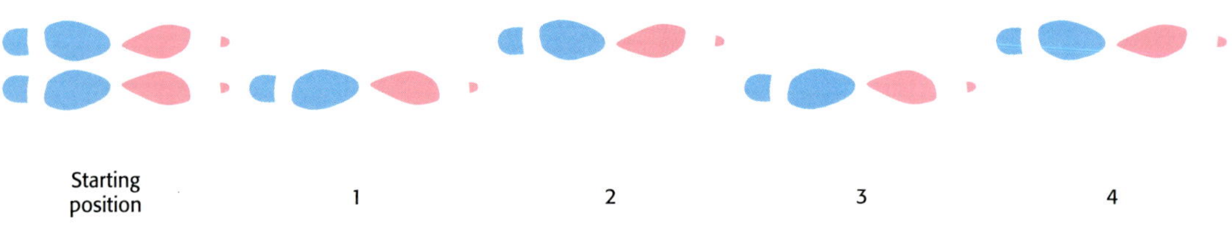

Paso Doble Steps – 1

Throughout these Paso Doble steps, assume that any walks are heel leads, with the exception of the 'Sur Place' steps on the spot and the stamps. Unlike the other Latin dances, the Paso Doble has no hip action.

Maintain good strong contact with your partner throughout, developing a dance relationship as well as an emotional relationship. The Paso Doble has a tendency to look feeble and weak if performed without obvious intention. Enjoy this opportunity to act! Men are strong matadors; ladies elegant and enticing capes!

Reflections on dance

'For the good are always the merry,
Save by an evil chance,
And the merry love the fiddle,
And the merry love to dance.'
William Butler Yeats (1865-1939)

Sur Place

Man begins facing down LOD.
Lady begins backing LOD.

1

Perform four steps on the spot, facing down LOD. The heels should be just off the floor. Lift your toes as you step – like a bullfighter rising onto his toes in order to perform. Try inhaling a deep breath to adopt the correct poise.
Perform four steps on the spot, backing LOD. The heels should be just off the floor. Lift your toes as you step.

2

1 2 3 4
R L R L
1 2 3 4
L R L R

3

4

Sur Place turning

Man begins facing down LOD.
Lady begins backing LOD.

Over counts 5, 6, 7, 8 the man initiates a 45° turn on the spot so that he now faces the wall and the lady faces the center.

Repeat the previous steps, while making a quarter-turn to face the wall.
5 6 7 8
R L R L

Repeat the previous steps, while making a quarter-turn to face the center.
5 6 7 8
L R L R

Paso Doble Steps – 2

Chassé capes

1

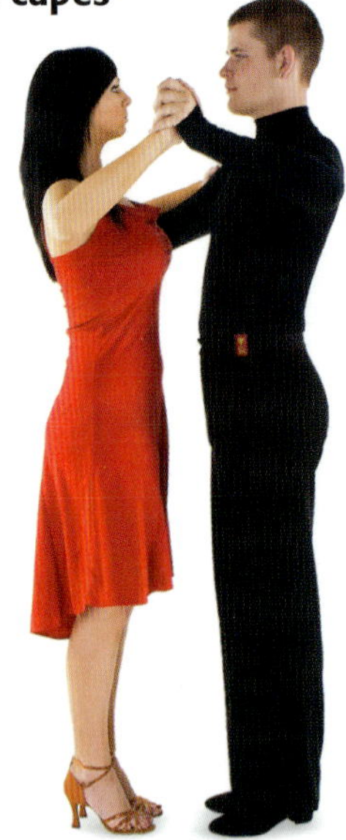

- Pick up your right foot and stamp beside your left foot on the flat.
- Pick up your left foot and stamp beside your right foot on the flat.

- Step your left foot to your left side in promenade position…
- Step your right foot to your right side in promenade position...

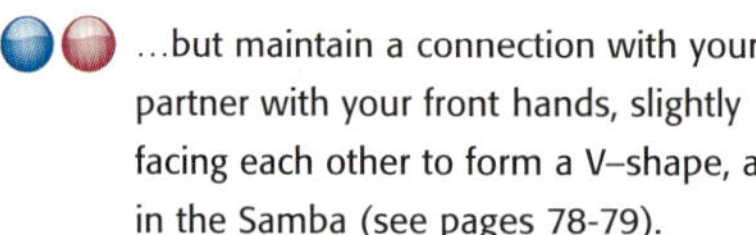

…but maintain a connection with your partner with your front hands, slightly facing each other to form a V–shape, as in the Samba (see pages 78-79).

- Step your right foot forward and across left along the LOD.
- Step your left foot forward and across right along the LOD.

Reflections on dance

'Dance is the hidden language of the soul.'

Martha Graham (1894–1991)

4

- (Chassé) Step your left foot to the left side, facing your partner.
- (Lock step) Step forward on your right foot along LOD.

- (Chassé) Close your right foot to your left.
- (Lock step) Left foot crosses behind.

5

- (Chassé) Step your left foot to your left side.
- (Lock step) Step forward on your right foot along LOD.

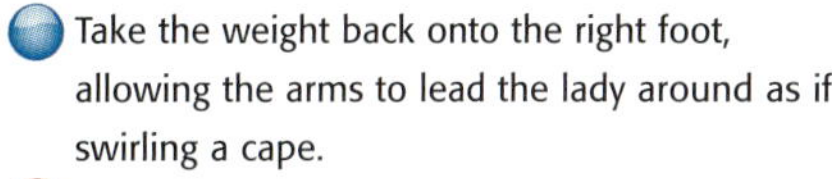

- Take the weight back onto the right foot, allowing the arms to lead the lady around as if swirling a cape.

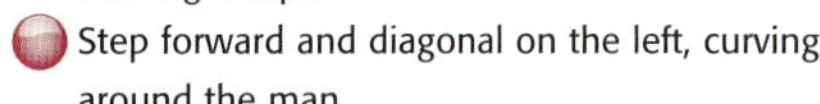

- Step forward and diagonal on the left, curving around the man.

- Lead lady round on count 7. Facing LOD, step forward on your left foot, allowing your body to continue turning to the left.
- Close your right foot to your left, making a three-quarter turn to face diagonal to the wall – the man should almost pull you round to this position. At this point you are imitating the cape!

- (Chassé) Step your right foot to the right side, facing center.
- (Lock step) Step forward on your left foot along LOD.

- (Chassé) Close your left foot to your right.
- (Lock step) Right foot crosses behind your left.

- (Chassé) Step your right foot to your right side.
- (Lock step) Step forward on your left foot along LOD.

- Repeat steps from count 6 but facing center, commencing on the left foot, and leading lady back round to the right.

Chassé capes repeats

2

- Take the weight back onto the left foot, allowing the arms to lead the lady round as if swirling a cape.
- Step forward and diagonal on the right, curving around the man.

3

- Lead the lady round on count 3: step forward on your right foot, allowing your body to continue turning to the right.
- Close your left foot to your right foot, making a three-quarter turn to face diagonal center. The man's movements should almost pull you round to this position.

4

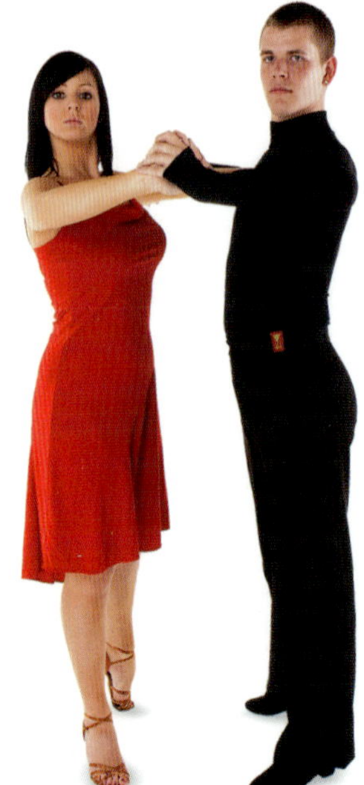

- Step your left foot to your left side, facing center.
- Step forward on your right foot along LOD.

&

- Close your right foot to your left.
- Your left foot crosses behind your right.

5

- Step your left foot to your left side.
- Step forward on your right foot along LOD.

- Repeat steps from count 6, commencing on the right foot, curving around the man, and closing left foot to right foot – having made a three-quarter turn to face diagonal to the center. Counts 2 3 Lock step 4 & 5

6

- Step your right foot forward and across left along the LOD.
- Step your left foot forward and across right along the LOD.

7

Close your left foot to your right foot.

Close your right foot to your left foot, turning to face your partner.

8

Hold.

You can now commence the Sur Place movement again, turning the stamps in the direction appropriate to your position on the dance floor.

Suggested choreography: Try performing one set of Sur Place, followed by the chassé cape. This sequence can be performed continuously.

Above: Man and lady are matador and cape for the duration of the Paso Doble!

Index

American Smooth 22
Astaire, Fred 22, 74

back break 84
baille con corte 40
ball-flat 17, 37
Ballroom 9, 10, 12, 18, 20-51, 53
Modern 22
Standard 22
ball-tap 36
beat 12
Brazil 74
Buenos Aires 40

Café de Paris 54
Carringford, Arthur 34
Castle, Irene and Vernon 34, 46
Castle Walk, the 46
Cha Cha 12, 53, 64-73
chassé 66, 68-69, 70
Chapouls 54
Charleston 46
Chmerkovskiy, Maksim 54
clothing 9, 10-11
Corté 44
Cuba 56, 64, 80
Cuban heel 10

dance holds 18-19, 39
Dolly Sisters 34
Dolly, Yansci (Jennie) 34

etiquette 9, 12-13

Flamenco 88
footwork 16-17, 58

Fox, Harry 34, 46
Foxtrot 12, 22, 34-39, 46
Slow 22, 24
Social (or Rhythm) 36-39

gaucho 40

heel lead 16, 90
hip-hop 6, 80
hips 17

jazz 22, 80
Jorrín, Enrique 64

Latin American 6, 9, 10, 18, 22, 52-95
lock step 51, 92-94

Mambo 64
Mambo-Rumba 64
Mardi Gras 53, 74
matador 88
Miranda, Carmen 74

New Yorks 60, 68
New York Theater 34

open face position 19
outside partner position 48, 62

Pan, Hermes 22
Papanti, Lorenzo 24
Paso Doble 53, 88-95
chassé capes 92-93, 94
posture 14-15
progressive chassé 50-51
promenade 36, 39, 78

Quicks 12
Quickstep 12, 22, 46-51

R&B 80
de Rhynal, Camille 22
Rio de Janeiro 74
Rogers, Ginger 11, 22, 74
Rumba 12, 53, 54, 56-63, 64, 66

Salsa 6, 12, 54, 64, 80-87
Samba 12, 53, 74-79
walks 78
whisk 77
Sambadrome 74
shoes 9, 10-11
shoulder to shoulder 62, 71, 73
side break 85
Slows 12
steps 16
Sur Place 90, 91

Tango 12, 18, 19, 22, 24, 40-45, 53
Argentine 40
rocks 43
walks 42
tempo 12
toe lead 16

underarm turn 71, 73, 86

Vienna 24
Volta 22

Waltz 6, 12, 22, 24-29, 56
Viennese 22, 30-33
warming up 14

Addresses and contacts

The dancers who appear in the photographs for this book were provided by:
Starlite School of Dance
Oakleigh, 204a New Hythe Lane
Larkfield, Kent ME20 6PT UK
Tel: +44 (0) 1732 843600
www.starlitedancing.com

Websites of general interest to dancers:
www.usabda.org
The home of USA DANCE, which acts as the United States' National Governing Body for ballroom dancing and DanceSport, subject to the statutes of the International DanceSport Federation and the US Olympic Committee.

www.ballroomdancingdirectory.com/index.php
This includes details of studios, dance teachers, clubs, and other dance-related services in the USA, Canada, and elsewhere.

www.dancesportmagazine.com
DanceSport magazine is the official publication of the American DanceSport Organization. Its website carries information about major US competitions (including the NY Dance Festival, the Florida Superstars, and the Virginia State DanceSport Championships), links to costume and shoe retailers, and other useful contacts.

The New York Dance Store (showroom and website) sells a comprehensive range of dance clothing, shoes, and accessories for adults and children:
www.nydancestore.com
Showroom address:
888, 8th Avenue, Corner 53rd Street
New York City, NY 10019
Tel: (212) 246 6212

The United States Imperial Society of Teachers of Dancing sets and administers tests and examinations in Ballroom, Latin, and other styles, and publishes a variety of training materials.
www.usistd.org

abc.go.com/primetime/dancingwiththestars/
The online home of the hit TV series, with news about shows and participants.

Websites relating specifically to Latin styles
www.latindancedirectory.com
This lists dance studios and schools, events, competitions, and clubs all over the world.

www.salsachicago.com
Another valuable source of information for salsa and Latin dancers.

www.salsapower.com
A site providing CD reviews, music downloads, details of festivals and shows, and other salsa-related listings.